# What others ar

I am not a writer, but I I
story. For over two dec
in all of life's situations. But with this life-threatening ordeal, Randy's
faith prevailed over the darkest fate. This book is a testament to that
spirit. I found myself swept up in his journey, realizing that we all can
discover that unique Voice within that not only quiets fears, but moves
mountains.

**Claude Grizzard Sr.**
*Chairman Emeritus, Grizzard Communications Group*

In captivating and compelling prose, Randy shares how losing his
physical voice to cancer led him to finding his real voice in life.
Sincere and full of good humor, he shares his toughest moments
and shows how profoundly they changed his view on suffering:
"Tragedy does not just take our voice, but paradoxically should
help us find our 'true' voice." He inspires courage and yet sincerity in the face of difficult situations that include a look at our
secret dark sides. Knowing Randy personally as a Board Member
of African Enterprise, I've known his unique physical voice and
perspective—and now I admire even more the "true" voice that
he's found for his life.

**Dr. Stephen Mbogo**
*International CEO, African Enterprise*

It's a revealing and personal story of redemption from soul-pain
and self-inflicted destruction. Randy opens himself up in ways that
every reader can relate to—and benefit from—as we each journey
deeper toward the healing power of grace and our own powerful
voice.

**Shannon D. Barnes**
*President, The EDGE Group*

What a wonderfully inspiring testimony of God's sufficient grace and faithfulness to Randy. His vulnerability and honesty allow us, as readers, to experience with him the journey of self-discovery, and more importantly, the discovery of Jesus in him. May we all find our true voice in Jesus, and may Randy's voice and testimony continue to touch countless people who are seeking God's Voice.

**Dr. Eugene Chung, MD**
*Radiation Oncologist*

I applaud the publication of your wonderful book! What makes your message so powerful is not just the revelation penned on its pages, but the fact that you are living it out by touching nations and changing lives of many around the world. Reading your book has not only built my faith but has also given me a fresh new appreciation of the workings of our Heavenly Father in the lives of His Children. Thank you for choosing to partner with World Harvest Africa as you say "yes" to the Voice from above!

**Reverend Ndjoli Iyanga**
*Regional Director, World Harvest Africa*

Life's challenges have a way of making us think more deeply about our lives—Randy's experience certainly did. His book is a testament to how radically God can work through the toughest times. As Randy describes reevaluating his entire life honestly and without pretense, it's a reminder to me that our challenges are often the hardest lessons to learn. . . and that in the end, our challenges expand our experience of God Himself.

**Rick Alvis**
*President/CEO, Wheeler Mission Ministries*

A heart-wrenching, but amazing journey through the life, career, and spiritual development of a successful Christian businessman. Randy has shared an incredible story of overcoming an impossible cancer; the miracle of healing; and a spiritual transformation from a shame-based Christianity to a grace-based follower of Christ.

**Gifford Claiborne**
*Director of Development, City Mission Ministries*

Randy has written from his heart. The language of the book communicates to the heart of all human beings, religious and non-religious alike. The story of his miraculous healing through reconstructive surgery is amazing. That doctors can recreate body parts using the basic ingredients that the Creator has generously provided is truly mind-boggling. Only the Creator could make that happen.

**Rosemary Wahu Mbogo, PhD**
*Senior Lecturer, Africa International University, Nairobi Founder,*
*ByGrace Children's Home, Kenya/ByGrace Trust, CA*


I have known Randy as his Pastor, but my privilege is to call him my friend. In the movie, *Gladiator*, Maximus said, "What we do in life echoes in eternity." Randy, I know your voice will continue to echo the amazing grace and hope of our Lord Jesus Christ both through your life and the words of this marvelous book.

**Pastor Scott Priest**
*Executive Associate Pastor, Restoration Fellowship Church*


*Finding My Voice* is both a spiritually and psychologically powerful true story of courage and hope. Few people have faced death and disabling disease on the level that Randy has, and fewer still come away with such a deep grasp of the difference between wishful thinking and true hope. Randy is one of those people.

This story of inspiration will encourage all those looking for comfort in the midst of their struggles. Randy's honesty and genuine faith in God is a refreshing example of what we can do when faced with impossible odds. God has not abandoned us to struggle alone in our problems, and reading this book will provide the support of a wise fellow traveler to all those feeling alone in theirs.

**Mark W Baker, PhD**
*Clinical Psychologist, Author of* Jesus, the Greatest Therapist Who Ever Lived

# FINDING
# MY VOICE

# FINDING MY VOICE

### A STORY
### OF GRACE, HOPE
### AND HEALING

## RANDY BREWER

**Big Snowy**
MEDIA

. . . . . . . . . . . .

Library of Congress Cataloging-in-Publication Data
Brewer, Randy Wayne, 1961—
*Finding My Voice: A Story of Grace, Hope and Healing*
Big Snowy Media
1. Religion
2. Spirituality

ISBN-13: 978-0-9852655-9-5

Printed in the United States of America

10 9 8 7 6 5 4 3 2 1

*This book is dedicated to the one true Voice . . .*
*the Word made flesh, my savior Jesus . . .*
*hope and grace made real.*

# CONTENTS

## ACKNOWLEDGEMENTS

**Special thanks:**

My siblings, Deb, Terry & Scott plus my niece, nephews and cousins who, while our family isn't perfect, still love and support each other, even in our craziness. To Jan & Matt Sommer for putting words to my many random thoughts.

**Thanks:**

Doctors Niels Kokot, Eugene Chung, Lindsay Reder, Jorge Nieva, Kevin McDonnell and many other medical professionals at Keck Medicine of USC and USC Norris Comprehensive Cancer Center; Doctors Marwan Fakih, Erminia Massarelli and the other medical professionals at City of Hope. My great friends Jeff & Miriam Riley, Jeudy Mom, Zack & Lyna Thoeun, Rea Barnes, Dr. Mark Baker, Kurt Vasquez and Shannon Barnes, plus my many friends in Japan and all over Asia and my international "kids" in Africa. I am blessed to have you all in my life. Thank you!

**Special recognition to my clients, friends and pastors:**

Rick & Julie Alvis, Steve Kerr, Ross & Kim Swihart, Eric & Robbin Burger, Phil Parsels, Pastor Scott Priest, Pastor Daniel Hanafi, and Pastor Stephanus Elia.

Venerated, iconoclastic Baptist minister Tony Campolo tells a story that bears repeating. He said that he was speaking at a church in the Northwest. As he was concluding his message, he felt the Holy Spirit's urging to offer a special, post-service prayer for anyone with a particular, pressing need. Among those who came to the front was a somewhat frail man who confided that he had late-stage cancer and desperately desired healing. Tony prayed fervently, going so far as breaking out a small vial of oil and anointing the afflicted man's head. Afterward, they hugged and went their separate ways.

Sometime later, Tony received a phone call. The woman on the other end of the line said she wanted to thank him for praying for her cancer-stricken husband following that church service up in the Northwest. She said it made such a huge difference and that God had answered Tony's prayer for healing. Assuming from her comment that the man was now in better health, Tony asked to speak with him. "I'm sorry," she said. "He recently passed away."

Sensing confusion in Tony's immediate response, the woman explained: After receiving the cancer diagnosis, her husband began to grow bitterly angry with God. He was looking forward to his impending retirement and wanted to see his children and grandchildren grow up. He felt God was taking away his heart's longings. As his disease progressed, he became more and more miserable and even belligerent with those around him.

But the woman went on to say that following his prayer time with Tony, something happened. A supernatural peace began to come over him. It seemed to be driven by a deep joy. In the days that followed, the woman said they read scripture together, prayed together and laughed together. She told Tony that she would always be grateful for his prayer of healing and would remember fondly the ensuing final weeks of her husband's life.

As Tony was caught up in a moment of silent contemplation, the woman made this final profound statement: "You see, Tony, he was healed, even though he wasn't cured."

The story my friend Randy Brewer tells in this book is also one of healing. Some of it is related to his physical health, but most of it is connected to his spiritual well-being. In the pages to follow, you will see what I mean even more.

The desire of most people, when they first face life's biggest crisis, is to escape unscathed. Some actually do. But those who confront painful predicaments head on and look for lessons to learn are the ones who can be our greatest, most trustworthy teachers. In that regard, Randy has become a master instructor. Because of what he has gone through and how he has handled it, his voice, for those of us who listen intently, will always be in our heads.

It's a voice that teaches us about transparency without embarrassment. Randy has been able to delve deeply into his early past and uncover and admit to family failings and personal foibles. Counselors will tell you it's good to process one's history to better handle the present. But Randy is bold enough to open up about what he has learned in later life—and is still learning, he would tell you—and that's what makes his voice a clarion call to life-long authentic Christianity.

That kind of honesty is missing today, particularly in pop culture and politics. People go to great lengths to shape and protect an image of correctness and perfection. Meanwhile, their enemies look for cracks in the façade, hoping to bring down their persona and defeat their positions.

This same kind of behavior in the Church is what musician and author John Fischer talked about in his classic book, *Real Christians Don't Dance!* (Bethany House, 1988).

Fischer asserts that many Christians try subtly or unabashedly to show they are worthy to be used by God. Fischer says, "The truth of the matter is we are not equal to the task. Those who try to be have no greater fate than Peter; the rooster crows over all our great claims of what we will do for God. Why? Because if a ministry depends on me, I will tend to present a false image of myself. If I am trying to be equal to the task, I am being dishonest about myself.

"This is why Paul goes on to say, 'Unlike so many, we do not peddle the word of God for profit. On the contrary, in Christ we speak before God with sincerity, like men sent from God' (2 Cor. 2:17 NASB). Real Christians are marked by sincerity—the whole truth about themselves and the whole truth about God. Real Christians stand before people the way they stand before God—transparent and vulnerable. Anything less is a dressed-up Gospel."

I have been privileged to work in tandem with Randy Brewer for the past ten years. The business that bears his name provides marketing methods and generates financial means for Gospel Rescue Missions all over North America. These are ministries that work with the most desperate and destitute individuals and families on our streets—those who have fallen through the rips in society's safety nets. Randy and his team have undergirded these missions to help countless thousands of poor and powerless people find help and hope.

I'm thankful that his voice will continue to be heard in the rescue mission world, but I'm also pleased that it will now be heard on another level in other arenas. It's a voice that reminds us that God's plans are perfect, his grace is boundless and his hope is eternal. Indeed, it's a strong voice of assurance for all who need healing.

**John Ashmen**
*President*
*Association of Gospel Rescue Missions*

# "...breathed...
# the breath
# of life"

Gen. 2:7

## Voice Breathed

Life. It emerged from the Creator's breath, turning chaos to order, dust to life.

And in those first few moments, what did Adam do?

He exhaled. He had taken in the Creator's life. And now breathed it out from his own being with his own unique expression.

Life in. Life out.

Life in, from the Creator. Life out, now particular to one person.

And with that breath—a Voice. That Voice coming from Adam, because of the breath energizing it, was the very Voice of God through him.

Right there in the quiet garden. The sound piercing the silence was a Voice breathed by God through Adam.

This was the Design. This was the Purpose, for not just Adam and Eve, but for every person.

We each are designed to breathe in, then out the breath of God. And in so doing we bring forth his Voice through our own unique identity.

Today, this may seem like a distant mystery. But it was and still is all too real.

That Voice becomes our voice.

That was the original intent.

His Voice breathed through us.

# CHAPTER 1

# YOU'LL NEVER SPEAK AGAIN

Twenty-seven doctors, ten hospitals, four countries—and everybody said the same thing. You should have your trachea and larynx removed. You'll breathe through a breathing hole. You'll probably be fed through a feeding bag. And you'll never speak again.

It was a rare throat cancer: adenoid cystic carcinoma. If I didn't have it removed through this radical surgery, eventually the cancer would grow, cut off my breathing, and I would die.

In many ways having the surgery—remaining alive with such a mutilated throat—would be much worse. The everyday functions of breathing and eating would be severely altered. But to lose the ability to speak—to lose my voice? I couldn't imagine a more dire fate.

My voice has always served me well. I'm in the communication business. I founded and own a direct marketing agency: Brewer Direct. For years, I have spoken to clients and colleagues every day in person and on the phone. Losing my voice would drastically limit my ability to conduct those affairs.

But even more distressing would be the loss of simple, personal communication: to look into someone's eyes, hear them, but not be able to answer; to want to genuinely respond, but limited only to silence.

My voice, like all voices, isn't just made up of words. There are inflections and meaning in the tones that come up from the heart. Oh, I could type or scratch out notes or send emails, but that is a different form of communication. Talking in some ways is like breathing - so spontaneous and effortless. It's a miracle convenience really, that our thoughts are instantaneously expressed in words. Sometimes it's like a floodgate opening, a release of ideas and feelings deep within the soul. Profound things come out of our mouths that we haven't even thought before. But they reach out and touch another with just the right meaning. Spoken words fill the moments with life. Without my voice, I would lose those spontaneous expressions.

When someone dies, we say, "We miss the sound of her voice." Or "I would just love to hear his voice again." Voice is so much more than a simple sound. There's only one person in the world who expresses like them: whose laughter, cries, passion, love and kindness come through in that one transcendent, unique voice. We miss the individual personality coming through. In some ways you could say the voice is the person at their core.

That's what I faced: not physical death, but the death of my own voice. A part of my being would be lost.

All of these thoughts raced through my mind: to hear, but not speak; to think, but not to express verbally; to have a relationship seemingly weighted to the other side. I would be like an out-of-balance wheel that doesn't spin true, bumping down the path of life out-of-whack.

A mute. That's what I would become. Restricted in all my inter-actions. Randy would still be inside. But could he really come forward? I'm not an artist. I certainly couldn't paint my feelings. I could still hug. But I couldn't look at someone face-to-face and tell them how I felt or how they made me feel.

We all know, the best communication is a two-way street. To be in a real relationship there needs to be give-and-take, a coming and growing together. That is how understanding happens. That is how love is expressed.

But without a voice, I would be cut off from that rich thorough-fare of interaction. No voice meant a severely restricted, less inti-mate expression of myself.

Chilling thoughts crept through me as I desperately contacted doctor after doctor across the globe. Surely there was something that could be done. Some magic bullet?

Strangely, at those terrifying moments when I contemplated my living death sentence, I had an equally disturbing thought: *Had I ever truly had a voice? What did I really have to say anyway?*

A voice isn't just a physical sound filling the air with noise. Two vocal chords vibrating. A voice is inextricably intertwined with the expression of the soul—our very being. A voice, at its core, is the per-son at their center. You could even argue that a voice is the person.

And mine was about to be lost.

My mind continued down into this abyss:

*Who was Randy the person with his own unique expression?*

*When I spoke, what was I really saying?*

*Was there some other voice lost deep down inside?*

# "Where are you?"

Gen 3:9

# Voice Lost

In the warmth of the garden came a cool voice.

It seemed true. It felt right.

This counterfeit promised, "You won't die, if you eat of the tree. Just the opposite. Your eyes will be opened, and you will be like God, knowing good and evil" (Gen. 3:5).

Ahhh ... to be like God. The thought was tantalizing. Could Adam and Eve actually be "like" the Voice that had breathed life into them? Their voice could take charge. It could have ultimate say.

Little did they know that the promise to gain control would cause them to lose life. Their voice of purity would be destroyed. Their voice of innocence would be lost.

But the temptation—"the delight to the eyes" and the desire "to make one wise"—proved to be too much. And they ate what was forbidden.

Immediately, they knew what they had done was wrong. They hid themselves.

God came looking for them. "Where are you?" This question wasn't just addressing where they were hiding physically. It identified something much deeper. "Where is the true you?"

The shame-filled Adam, stripped of his God-given identity, answered truthfully, "I hid myself."

And this is the curse for all people. In our own craving for control, we become lost. Our true voices—our true selves—are hidden from the one who is the Author of Life.

# CHAPTER 2

# SHHH... FAMILY SECRETS

My dad didn't like noise.

He sat at the dinner table with a fly swatter. If my siblings and I got out of line, he smacked us with it.

I wasn't a hyperactive child. Actually, I was a good kid. When I look back now, my behavior that triggered my father's reaction was no different than that of any other ordinary child. But when you're whacked for simply expressing yourself normally, you learn two things: not to express yourself and, well, not to be normal.

We all know the concept called "the family secret." It refers to some dark act in the family that nobody talks about. It's hidden in the family basement. Eventually it may come out and bring with it turmoil, heartache and even rage. But usually it's more insidious than that. It expresses itself through strange and sometimes out-of-left-field dysfunctions.

The fact is a family secret likes to keep itself as a secret. It wants to dodge in and out of the shadows of a family, within the souls of the individual members. The secret knows that if it were brought into the light of day, it could be destroyed.

Family secrets never want to be unveiled. They want to stay behind the curtain, pulling their destructive strings. The dark force that caused the family secret in the first place is a controlling puppet-master, and the family its marionette puppets.

In my family growing up, there wasn't just one single, big skeleton in one closet. There were layers of dysfunction. Secrets were twisted inside secrets, inside secrets. It was Pandora's box, unopened. And my three siblings, my mother, my father and I lived together inside that box.

My dad was a playboy when he married my mom. He was 20 years older. His infidelity continued after the marriage, but this, of course, he tried to keep a secret. All we knew was that women would call the house.

My mom came into the marriage with her own disruptive past. Her father had been an alcoholic, and she had dropped out of high school to take care of him. She also got pregnant at 16 and put the baby up for adoption.

When these two found each other, Dad was a dry drunk, had been married and divorced and was a secret womanizer. Mom was pregnant a second time by another man.

This all was swept under the proverbial rug. From the beginning, the entangled dysfunctions were there.

Secrets and unresolved wrongdoing tend to prompt the people who hold them to overcompensate. Those in on the secret create an exterior life that appears filled with light and goodness.

It's like painting over rotten boards. Whitewashing.

The heavy weight of darkness had to have a counter-balance. Most humans can't live with themselves if they've morally failed over and over again. The shame is overwhelming.

Shame has its own dysfunctional rules. As the bad actions pile up, a never-ending diatribe of condemnation is piled on. People go into a psychological state of shock. They can't deal with the guilt of all their wrong acts. The evil to which they've succumbed has to be atoned. The bad has to be rectified.

So they overcorrect and can become overachievers in right living. They not only welcome, but they become zealous in observing the rules. In short, they become hyper-law-keepers. They embrace a performance-based religion.

My mom and dad defaulted to this. My dad became an assistant Christian education pastor at a legalistic church. He ran vacation Bible school. My mother went right along with it, playing the role of dutiful wife. We went to church together as a family. We attended church potlucks and picnics. We weren't Chreasters—just Christmas and Easter church-goers. No, we immersed ourselves in Sunday school, summer camps and special events. If the church was organizing it, the Brewers were there—the whole family of whitewashed boards lined up.

Back at home, behind closed doors, the dysfunctions continued. The whitewash washed off.

One of the ironic offshoots was that my mother constantly cleaned. This wasn't just your normal housekeeping. Once everything was dusted and the dishes done, then she would wash the walls and doors. Everything had to be scrubbed.

As I look back now, I realize it was her obsessive effort to maintain order. It actually was indicative of a person who felt somewhere deep inside that everything was out of control. Such is the nature of a shame-filled, legalistic mindset. The person is forever feeling inadequate. So they compensate. Someone can feel dirty on the inside, guilty for past and present sins, and they dysfunctionally react by attempting to "clean up" the physical world around them.

Such was my mother's compulsion. And as a child I was literally swept up in her obsession. To this day I can't leave the house without making my bed and having everything tidy.

The hypocrisy in my home continued endlessly. It was an incessant cycle of toxic shame and trumped-up virtue. A fly on the wall would have seen this pretense expressed in our day-to-day lives. Mom and Dad presented a cleaned-up, tranquil life to the world. However, at home Mom scrubbed away as if extricating nagging transgressions; and Dad bellowed, attempting to maintain order. The underlying driving force was constraint. It was the epitome of human effort to correct and control all that was uncontrollable—namely their own shortcomings. Tragically, it wasn't so much that what they did *was wrong*, it was that they felt—at their core—they *were wrong*.

I was force-fed this corrupted worldview. As I moved into adulthood, I characterized myself as "repulsive." What a poisonous word. What a tragic label. I perceived myself as fundamentally tarnished. I was damaged goods. Hopelessly irredeemable.

In all fairness, my mom and dad were victims of their own families' generational misdeeds. Alcoholism, homelessness, abuse, crime and womanizing ran through our family for generations. They were obviously unaware of the grace and mercy available that could free them from their own tainted upbringings—the twisted patterns that had been imprinted on them.

Sadly, the true message of grace somehow did not get through. It just wasn't there. Christianity was an edict-based religion to them. It was all about keeping the rules and keeping up appearances. When you failed morally, there were punishments to be dealt out. Most of these were self-inflicted—the twin swords of condemnation and shame.

The additional carnage in this approach to life is that true needs aren't truly met. Real human feeling is not only shunned, it actually can be attacked. My dad certainly didn't meet my mother's deeper wants and wishes. He established his own bedroom, bathroom and TV room—his own kingdom within our home. His idea of a relationship with a woman was so stilted based on his years of using women as objects. Because of this, my mother was left in an emotional vacuum.

So she attempted to have those needs fulfilled in and through her children. My siblings and I became intertwined with her quest for that missing connection. In short, she relied on us to prop her up. She was a child leaning on children for support. Instead of her feeding us, we had to feed her. Her emotional needs became our problem, but of course, as children, we were certainly not equipped to deal with this. How could a two-, seven- or even 12-year-old overcome?

This all may sound like armchair psychology. But let me assure you, what happened imbedded itself deep in my psyche. Being raised in this dysfunctional world squelched me as a person. I, like all children growing up, wanted to be carefree, transparent and open. Yet the vice of condemnation and shame squeezed out all that carefreeness.

I learned early on to put up my own walls. To literally hide. There was a tight space between the dryer and the wall in the laundry room. I turned on the dryer and hid there. The warmth and hum of the dryer calmed my mind. As a child, I desperately attempted to find a measure of solace. In junior high, I put locks on my bedroom door. I was afraid to answer or talk on the telephone.

I became an actor, in a sense. I quickly learned my role in this strange theater called my home. We all followed an unwritten, but no less imposing, script.

Exploration for a child is critical. And that exploration doesn't just entail physically investigating one's surroundings. It also entails being allowed to say what one's thinking. There's a sort of healthy trial-and-error in this. A resonance with the world occurs. Kids are like a person standing in a canyon. They let out their voice and it comes echoing back. Some sounds reverberate within. Others don't resonate. But this process can and should be very organic.

In my house, the words that went out often came back with a sharp reprimand. Most of the rebukes were not logical. However, in my child's mind, there was a rationality to it: *I said this, and then this terrible thing happened. I'm not sure why, but I guess I better not say or express that anymore.*

The overarching effect was that the unresolved failures and short-comings in my family pulled me down into their darkness. They were saying, *No, Randy, don't live out in the light. Trust me. Light is bad. Living down here in the grotto of life is much better. Restrict. Restrict.*

I learned to stay in the shadows. I not only learned not to express outwardly, I also learned not to feel inwardly.

However, there was that hypocritical counterweight operating in my family. The painting over rotten boards continued, and I became very good at it, just like my parents. In fact, in my unaware state, I actually thought of myself as the whitewash itself. I began to believe the fake goodness about myself.

The family secrets were so egregious that it was actually easier just to ignore them. The secrets wanted to remain secrets even to me. More importantly—and here's the most disturbing thing—they wanted the true me to remain a secret from myself.

The darkness that brought out that corruption in the first place knows something that actually terrifies it. It understands that if a person ever truly becomes a real person, its gig is up.

No, the puppet master behind the dark secrets has an ultimate goal. He never wants a person to be an authentic being. A unique individual is an anathema. He'll do anything to make people prisoners in their minds and souls. He actually loves the torment of someone *not being* a someone. He wants that person to be consumed by the worst within them. But then, he loves when a person tries to escape by offering a false representation of themselves to the world.

Oh, they can walk around and make an appearance to the world like all is not only okay, but fabulously filled with goodness. It's a performance-based faith, focused on the external self. However, if the exterior veneer were peeled back, you would see an infestation of spiritual disease, like termites in the soul.

No, I learned within the dysfunction of my youth to hide, and to create an appearance. However, I was largely unaware of this emotional bait-and-switch that was operating in my life. I was a fully functioning person on one hand, but a severely broken-down being on the other.

To say that my voice growing up was squelched would be an understatement. Deep down, in the basement of my soul, layers of dysfunction held me prisoner. They had me right where they wanted me. It felt like I was held captive, even tortured, by a sadistic jailer. And he would let me out, if only I continued to pretend to present myself to the world as a liberated man.

But this free man was not free at all. Behind the secrets, the warden—that puppet-master—was pulling the strings. He even controlled the string that made my jaw move. I actually could speak, but what I spoke was not me. It wasn't my authentic voice on the stage of life.

How very strange that I would now have throat cancer. I, the wooden puppet, was about to have a laryngectomy. The puppet wouldn't even be able to pretend to have a voice.

# "...count the stars..."

Gen. 15:5

# VOICE OF PROMISE

It was a promise as vast as the stars.

That Voice of promise came to a wandering soul -- unremarkable in his stature or standing in the world.

However, he had one profound attribute at the core of his being. He believed God.

Abraham did not have some flip, Pollyannaish view of faith. No, he was convinced of a certain future, even though the reality of his present situation was diametrically opposed.

Though he and Sarah were old and childless, he believed they would usher in a lineage that would change the world.

This belief was based on a resounding Voice. "The word of the Lord came to Abraham in a vision: 'Now look to the heavens, and count the stars, if you are able to count them.... So shall your descendants be'" (Gen. 15:5).

That Voice of promise changed everything. It reached into the heart of his circumstances and said, "Another reality is possible. Trust Me." While he lived in monochrome, the Voice promised a world of rich, vibrant color.

That Voice speaks to every human down through history and to us today. It says no matter what you see in front of you or even what you've done in the past, right now there is a promise held for you as vast as the galaxies above.

We each are capable of triumph. Our purpose can be fulfilled. Our course can be altered. If we but listen to that Voice. It speaks not in platitudes but in possibilities—not in clichés but with distinct certainty.

As we look up to the night sky and listen, we hear that Voice calling. It whispers a promise as real, uplifting and world-changing as the very stars themselves.

# CHAPTER 3

# THE EARACHE THAT WOULDN'T STOP

I t was a three-year earache. And it wasn't some little twinge or blockage. It was a throbbing piercing agony. Sometimes I would double over in pain.

To find what was causing this misery, a host of doctors ran me through a litany of tests. An ear-nose-and-throat doctor thoroughly examined my ears. No abnormalities. Next they administered allergy tests. Nothing. They ordered a CT scan of my nasal passages. All clear. They put me on a restricted diet. It didn't help. I went to a chiropractor to adjust my spine. No reprieve. Doctors even advised I have a tooth extracted, thinking it pressed on some nerve. Again, no relief.

This went on for months. After all this prodding and poking, I had no diagnosis. No resolution. This vacuum left me—a fixer, a problem-solver, a doer—utterly frustrated, especially as the throbbing continued day in and day out. The only thing I learned through the testing was characterized by one doctor who said, "You have the health of a 20-year-old." That would have been ironically funny, except that the mind-numbing pain was no laughing matter.

Finally, I suggested to my doctor, "Why don't you do an MRI of my throat?" This was a stretch. After all, the pain was in my ear, not my throat. But he ran the test. And then the call came. "The doctor wants to see you. Today."

The MRI revealed a distinct mass, entangled and hidden in the complex structures of the larynx or voice box. It was cancer. The earache had a source. The pain was actually due to a nerve that runs from the throat up to the ear called Arnold's nerve. The expression of the pain was in the ear, even though the problem was in the throat.

Fortunately, my doctor was immediately able to get me an appointment with Dr. Niels Kokot at Keck Medicine/ USC—one of the top head-and-neck surgeons in the U.S. He ran more tests and did a biopsy. They discovered not just any cancer. It was a rare form called Adenoid cystic carcinoma. This malignancy does not respond to traditional cancer treatments. That meant no chemo. Given what I'd seen others go through, that was in some ways a relief. However, the alternative was a radical surgery.

Normally they can resect the larynx and pharynx to maintain normal throat functions. But this tumor was too large and was wrapped around those structures in such a way that there was only one possible treatment: complete removal of the larynx.

Finally, the diagnosis was confirmed. It was a relief to know what the problem was; it was devastating to know the treatment.

Strangely, my initial reaction was fatalistic acceptance. Somewhere in my spirit I felt I had earned this. The tyrannical voices of condemnation and shame reared their heads with a relentless cacophony: *You deserve to be dead. You had this coming. You're finally reaping what you've sown. The corruption within has finally manifested itself.* On and on they droned, echoing through my spirit, with wave after noxious wave.

The tyranny from my childhood of a thousand rebukes, which I had managed to keep dormant, mounted a full-on insurrection. Whatever defenses I had put up in my life to keep those attacks at bay were being overrun by the enemy.

I tried to keep those dark voices in check through staying busy with life and work. But even in that earthly hustle, I had horrific thoughts come to mind. For instance, I would open a garage door and sense that someone was there to kill me. I lived in the sunshine of the real world. But then, a thought would come like a dark nightmare that jolts you from sleep. Only I would be fully awake when these alarming apparitions would come! I knew rationally they were figments of my dark imagination.

But this horrendous cancer wasn't an illusion. The death I envisioned was finally upon me, and it was a most horrific form. This would be, in some ways, a living death. Those aberrant cells, growing out of control, were all too real. And it only took the simplest bait-and-switch for my damaged soul to deduce that I, Randy Brewer, was malignant at my core.

Such is the nature of toxic shame. It lies there like an incurable virus. No remedy can touch it. And to make matters worse, given the right circumstances, it comes out with full fury. Any human attempt to purge oneself from it is met with a cynical scoff, "You can't get rid of me. I'm here to stay, because what I am is who you really are." Like my cancer, shame wraps itself around a healthy organ and takes over, squeezing out all life. Condemnation is the same. It entwines itself around the human spirit, strangling the true breath of life.

Many are so steeped in shame and condemnation they actually think they are part and parcel to the human experience. I actually had people tell me, "You better figure out what you did to deserve this." Thinking rooted in condemnation says that for every negative outcome there must be a negative cause. Bad actions lead to bad consequences. Of course that's true in many circumstances. But what if there isn't a direct link? What if someone experiences a negative reality and there is no cause-effect corollary?

Jesus addressed this exact predicament head-on:

> As He passed by, He saw a man blind from birth. And His disciples asked Him, "Rabbi, who sinned, this man or his parents, that he would be born blind?" Jesus answered, "It was neither that this man sinned, nor his parents; but it was so that the works of God might be displayed in him. We must work the works of Him who sent Me as long as it is day; night is coming when no one can work. While I am in the world, I am the Light of the world." When He had said this, He spat on the ground, and made clay of the spittle, and applied the clay to his eyes, and said to him, "Go, wash in the pool of Siloam" (which is translated, Sent). So he went away and washed, and came back seeing. Therefore, the neighbors, and those who previously saw him as a beggar, were saying, "Is not this the one who used to sit and beg?" Others were saying, "This is he," still others were saying, "No, but he is like him." He kept saying, "I am the one." So they were saying to him, "How then were your eyes opened?" He answered, "The man who is called Jesus made clay, and anointed my eyes, and said to me, 'Go to Siloam and wash'; so I went away and washed, and I received sight" (John 9:1-11).

Jesus not only wanted to heal the blind man, but he also wanted to underscore a vital truth within God's kingdom: It was neither that this man sinned, nor that his parents sinned; but it was so that the works of God might be displayed in him. Jesus rose above the normal cause-effect logic of fallen humankind that leads to condemnation. He abolished the blame game.

People love to point fingers at others and at themselves. Of course, it's the nature of the dark spirits of the universe to stir up blame. The Bible describes Satan as, "...the accuser of our brethren...he who accuses them before our God day and night" (Rev. 12:10). Accusation goes hand-in-glove with condemnation.

But when Jesus healed the blind man he condemned false condemnation. The finger of shame and guilt no longer pointed. Like every human being, the parents and the blind man both sinned. We all do. But Jesus couldn't see the sin. He only could see his redemption of it.

Isn't that one of the hallmarks of grace? It's a surprise. It's unexpected. It doesn't connect the dots of our failures and chart a course to hopeless guilt. As only God can, he recognizes our shortcomings, but also sets us free because that debt has been paid through the blood of Christ. Like the blind man whose sight was restored, we who are swept up in the goodness of grace, suddenly grasp what God has been seeing all along: Jesus' humility poured out for the world for God's good purpose.

People often express, "He's finally getting what he deserved. I hope he learns from this." A legalistic mindset focuses entirely on cause-effect. You break the law; you pay the price. But the grace mindset opens another dimension. You break the law; he pays the price; and your eyes are forever opened to a new understanding of truth. You develop a humility of spirit, an empathy for others and an abounding love. In God's economy, the riches that come from grace is something much richer. Like the blind man, our response is utter humility and unending joy.

Unfortunately, I missed this understanding in my upbringing. When I was diagnosed with cancer, my default was to re-embrace the idea that it was my fault. I believed I deserved cancer.

This was the voice coming through. This was the voice that echoed within, even as they were about to surgically remove my physical voice. These were the death-tones of my reality, and I could not escape them. For those voices were not of this physical world. They were deep down inside me, emanating from a dark spiritual domain.

Yes, I was about to lose my earthly voice—have it cut out. Yet those voices of condemnation and shame could in no way be removed.

Or could they?

> # "The voice of the Lord is powerful…"
>
> Ps. 29:4

# Voice of Thunder

He was a shepherd boy who spent many hours alone in a field, just listening.

And in those quiet moments, David was hearing what could be.

He emerged from that obscure life, a young man with no doubts. The reason he could slay Goliath was not because of his own superiority. It was that he believed God could do it through him.

To David, the Voice was power, possibility and unbounded strength.

This indomitable spirit pulsing through him allowed David not just to defeat a giant. He went on to establish a kingdom.

But he wasn't just a military general consumed with victory. In and through all of his conquests (and inevitable setbacks), he played a harp and wrote psalms. He tapped into the inner strength that comes by pouring out one's heart and receiving a renewed, heartfelt passion.

He wrote about this power, capturing and comparing it to a monstrous thunderstorm, rising in the west over the Mediterranean and breaking with full force across the mountains and deserts of Lebanon and Israel. He described it as "the voice of the Lord."

This was so much more than depicting a weather event. No, this was a physical picture of the power he felt inside.

It was the power that could "break cedars," make nations "skip like a calf," "shake the wilderness" and cause "deer to calve." But above all, it caused him to exclaim, "Glory!"

And in witnessing this mighty, physical act, David was reminded of one overriding principle: "The Lord will give strength to His people."

This was a powerful reminder of the true Voice of thunder that God desires to unlock within each of us.

CHAPTER 4

# MASKS

I was the popular kid at my church. That was ironic, because behind that effusive personality was a deep shyness. The hiding I did as a child, in the space by the dryer, translated into a hiding of my true self.

However, if you were to meet me then, the withdrawn person wasn't apparent. In my early teens, I remained in a concealed state. I started to play music in the church band. At first, I was timid and hid behind the drums. Then something clicked. I discovered that when I asserted the smallest blip of personality and leadership, the other teenagers noticed me.

For a kid who had thought of himself as unworthy, unnecessary, even repulsive—I lapped up their attention. It energized me. Suddenly, I was the guy people wanted to be around. I discovered that I didn't just like being the person out in front—the pied piper of all things fun—I also could relate to the hidden rhythms of those around me. A troubled soul can instinctively spot trouble in another. I was both effusive and empathetic. And for kids going through the trials of their teen years, I became the person to whom they could relate.

Looking back, I see the grand irony of this. I was an ally to my friends, yet I was the one in dire need of support. The helper required the most help.

God established a foothold in my life. Yes, my parents had major shortcomings that deeply affected me. However, I'm grateful they pointed me in the direction of faith. They obviously lacked the ability to love perfectly, but by taking me to church, they made a way for me to experience the love of God.

This causes me to marvel at God's ways. We see enormously flawed people in the Bible. And yet God moved in and through them. He fans the tiniest spark of faith and nurtures it to its fullest flame. God looks at the heart's motives, not the flesh's failure.

The truth took hold. I didn't move into my teenage years and suddenly rebel and abandon my faith. Instead I gravitated toward it. I embraced it—at least the form of it that I had been taught.

I later learned how stilted my understanding of faith was. Despite my lack of understanding, a seed was planted. My parents could have easily abandoned faith altogether. Whether their reasons were good or bad, my parents brought us to church and exposed us to the truth. And God used it.

From an early age, God infused me with spiritual yearning. I read the Bible so much as a child, that later my parents gave me my grandmother's Bible. Looking back, I can say that yearning was by his grace. Despite the weeds that had grown up around me, something altogether pure and good was there.

I take no credit for it. God imprinted me. Like a master gardener, he brought his vineyard, known as Randy Brewer, to fruition. Such is the nature of God. He knows the spiritual DNA that rests within. DNA is simply coding—the architectural designs of something still to be fully built and realized. But those designs are masterful. Back then I wasn't aware of any of this. Now, I can watch the beauty of the process. And I can see his protection. Despite the slings and arrows of outrageous fortune that attacked me, and despite my own innumerable shortcomings, he kept me on his course. He patiently watered, weeded and waited for what was to bloom.

His devotion to me is humbling. If it were up to me, I would have abandoned myself. There is the crux of toxic shame: the person hates the person they are. It is what Paul said, "The good that I would do, I do not do. Oh wretched man that I am"(Rom. 7:19).

However, at that point the pure plant and the abnormal weeds grew together. Yes, the kids loved me. But I also received the attention and admiration from the kids. I received a lot of praise, a sugar pill given my bitter upbringing. I gladly ate it up.

I came out of my shell—at least on the surface. The doer went into overdrive with ever-increasing fervor. I had learned to be an over-compensator. I embraced my new identity with a consuming intensity. I made things happen.

As I moved into my 20s I became a promoter for Christian rock bands. That agent role spilled over into the secular world. I managed Asian rock bands, I brokered record deals and set up gigs at the best LA nightclubs. All musicians want a venue to play in, and I was the guy to get it for them. The bands loved me, which fed my false sense of love. I realize now I was attempting to nourish an insatiable hunger. Outside effort was spawned by inside turmoil.

My brother Scott—a fellow victim in our dysfunctional home— got involved fairly early with drugs and alcohol. (Thank God, he's been set free and today serves as a pastor.) But back then it was painful to watch these addictions consume him. I feared drugs and alcohol because of how it destroyed my brother, father and grandparents. Though I went to countless nightclubs, I didn't succumb to those temptations. Professionally, I moved from being a youth pastor to working with non-profits through various fundraising agencies. As a fully focused promoter—the guy who made things happen—I became very successful.

It wasn't all business. I also helped homeless missions grow donor support. It was satisfying to assist these outstanding ministries in their efforts to provide for the hurting. Beneath my noble efforts, though, my faulty foundation gave way. Despite my success, my insecurities led to authoritative behavior that was rude and demanding. I wanted to be called *Mr. Brewer*. A colleague even observed, "Randy, you only order special meals on an airplane because you want to hear your name being called." The reticent boy who hid in the gap by the dryer wanted to be a self-reliant, confident man for all to see. Insecurity, by definition, loves to overreact. What you are not, you want to prove you are.

I couldn't prop up from the outside something missing on the inside. It's the polar opposite of how God designed the human psyche. Individuality originates in the heart, and from the heart the world around us is influenced and changed. However, I couldn't or wouldn't embrace this. I had a false sense of being important. That had stoked the engine of my being. Throughout my early career, I kept fueling that fire. I wanted to look the part. I literally drove a sleek sports car.

I isolated myself in endless travel. My condo was not a respite but a pit stop. I always wanted back out on the track. There was little to stop this unhealthy course. My obsession with work led to my clients' success, and for that I'm grateful. But I was coming apart. This spilled over into all my personal relationships. I had acquaintances, but not abiding friends. Why should I? True friendship meant transparency, even vulnerability. I would have none of that. At work, my relationships weren't much better.

I hired and managed poorly. Why attend to those around me when I prioritized attending to myself?

This went on for nearly two decades. I was adrift on a sea—a cesspool really—of false pretense. I began propping up my deep-seated insecurities with distractions, compulsions and a false sense of importance. I engaged in several misadventures, finding myself asking God like David did: "Do not remember the sins of my youth…" (Ps. 25:7).

I understand now that I was on a fool's errand. I was trying to fill a bucket with holes. Theologians and philosophers refer to this as a God-shaped vacuum.

The French philosopher Pascal characterized it this way: "What else does this craving, and this helplessness, proclaim but that there was once in man a true happiness, of which all that now remains is the empty print and trace? This he tries in vain to fill with everything around him, seeking in things that are not there the help he cannot find in those that are, though none can help, since this infinite abyss can be filled only with an infinite and immutable object; in other words, by God himself" (Blaise Pascal, *Pensées VII*, 425).

All my striving came to a head in Mexico. I was in my early 40s. Even though I had steered clear of alcohol up to this point, I binged, trying to keep up with 22-year-olds. In trying to be the coolest, I had become valueless. You could even say I was nauseatingly lukewarm as a person. My faith, at that time, was tepid as well. My hypocrisy was blatantly obvious to everyone, including myself.

I was adrift. I didn't know where I belonged. This was when I began to become aware of the secrets that dwelled in the basement of my psyche.

I no longer could be the wanna-be teenager, the guy who had it together or the obsessed workaholic. The song of life was calling me. I made a decision to shed my sophomoric identity. I no longer needed, nor wanted, the bachelor pad or the sports car. I didn't want to be the rock band promoter and spend my weekends in smoky nightclubs. I discarded those pursuits. I began remodeling my home from the inside out. I got rid of the sports car. Despite developing many friends from the bands I promoted, I said goodbye to music promotion.

This external purging, while good in one sense, was still peripheral. I discarded the external trappings of a man, but I was still imprisoned on the inside.

The light that had led me to clean house called me to discard the tarnished image of myself. But how? Was there something greater? It was time to discover what it meant to be a child of God and be embraced by him.

It was at this time of spiritual renewal that I took another hit. At the age of 42, I lost my job. It was a complicated situation. Yes, I had made mistakes. But I also was swept up in some broader corporate issues. It was a punch in the gut. The absence of work, which was my identity, forced me to examine a lot of issues. Because I wasn't fully immersed in and distracted by activity, I had to look at myself. Who was I without work?

Everything in my work-obsessed world came to a screeching halt. I was like a race car suddenly taken off the track. Ironically, when I finally got back in the car, I found myself actually wanting to slow down. I didn't want to go as fast as I could. I explored the lower, slower gears. In fact, for a time, I didn't even want to go back out on the track. The thrill, or rather the obsessive need for speed, was throttled.

As I slowed down, I began to see people not as entities to figure out and even control, but as the precious, unique individuals God created. A crack had been opened, and I saw glimpses of light. It wasn't anything revolutionary. I began to discover a new part of myself.

Exterior change can be a good thing. But for a guy like me who was raised to present a glossed-over, false representation of himself, just changing my actions wasn't the path to a lasting freedom. It was good to slough off the trappings of counterfeit power and purpose, but I wanted something more.

Even before I was diagnosed with cancer, I experienced a flawed world crumbling around me. My pursuit of happiness and trying to carve out an identity through work, a sports car, distraction and trumped-up self-importance didn't work. The identity I obsessively tried to create suddenly became exposed for what it truly was: counterfeit. In short, I lost myself. The weekend of attempted revelry in Mexico actually exposed the vanity of my obsessive pursuits.

While God isn't to blame for loss, he is the one who wants to turn it for good. Because he is love itself, he wants to fill the void caused by our losses. He wants to restore what we have unknowingly or overtly ruined.

He goes one step further. While he might restore the actual thing we've wrecked, he adds to it. He does "above and beyond what we could ask or think." As only the one whose "ways are not our ways" can do, he fills the void with an understanding of the most precious thing in the universe: an unbridled revelation of himself and a more expansive awareness of ourselves.

He turns our negative things into his positives. This doesn't mean God (or I) condone wrongdoing in order that his goodness can come. No, the Bible is very clear on this. "Are we to continue in sin that grace may increase?" (Rom. 6:1). Of course not. But it does mean that even in the darkness that is caused by our own missteps and the failings of those around us, he is ready, indeed eager, to pour out goodness undeserved.

This is exactly what I experienced. It came in the form of a surprise. I can't say I stumbled upon it. I can most assuredly assert that it purposefully came after me. This cache of riches that suddenly was revealed has a simple name: grace.

Grace is central to the Christian faith. Perhaps the most famous song in all of Christianity is "Amazing Grace." Most Christians know the basic tenets of grace. I heard about the truth of grace growing up. But it's a funny thing about truth. Truth has to be known. It can't just sit as a sterile principle, or some statutory law. The Bible says, "...and you will *know* the truth, and the truth will make you free" (John 8:32).

I had heard, I had read and I had even spoken about the concept of grace. But I had not *known* it. The word "to know" in the Greek is *ginōskō*. It means "to know and to be known." Knowing isn't just understanding facts. True knowing is to grasp a greater something, or to be more specific, to know a greater someone. Simultaneously, we better know ourselves. As we gain more knowing of him, we gain more knowing of ourselves.

The idea of grace, while talked about in my upbringing, didn't live within me. It wasn't a spring of life. The concept of grace was wrapped around all that other refuse in my childhood. It, like so much of the other white-washing, fell into that category of pretense.

But it's the nature of grace to be persistent. Or it's the nature of the one who is grace incarnate not to give up. God wants us to embrace him, the one who has already embraced us. He wants us to know his life-giving truths, like we know an intimate friend.

After nearly two decades of adult life and two decades of life within my tumultuous family—my dissatisfaction was revealing itself. The partying in Mexico was a wake-up call. I could see that something was wrong. But I wasn't sure how to pursue or grasp what was right. So I sought out answers from multiple sources. Understanding came—some quickly, some over time—with the help of counseling, mentoring by other mature Christians, searching and God's gentle revelations.

A fresh understanding of grace was emerging. The message that once was dead was suddenly alive: "And He has said to me, 'My grace is sufficient for you, for power is perfected in weakness.' Most gladly, therefore, I will rather boast about my weaknesses, so that the power of Christ may dwell in me" (2 Cor. 12:9).

A switch was flipped. I didn't just see light. I saw an unfathomable array of all the colors within light itself. Physicists explain that white light is actually made up of a spectrum of color. When white light hits a prism, it is split into that rainbow of colors, based on their differing wavelengths. Grace, you could say, is the prism that separates God's light into a rainbow of colors, the multitudinous wavelengths of God himself. I was now seeing aspects—or colors—of him I hadn't seen or known before. This is the nature of grace. Grace brings out the color—or combination of colors—within a person.

Despite my weaknesses from my childhood and throughout my adult life, I watched power made manifest despite my weaknesses. That doesn't mean God intended or caused all the wrongdoing in my upbringing. Rather, he operated in and through them to turn them from dark to light, from colorless to color-filled.

Many helped me better understand grace. I began attending a church where, thankfully, no one was impressed with me and my abilities or successes. They wanted relationships based on who I was at my core. Pastor Scott Priest provided a new understanding of grace that I had never heard. The message of grace washed me of my need-to-perform mentality. I began ridding myself of self-adoration. Performance-based faith ("If you do, you will get") was exposed for what it was.

I felt rest. I didn't need to do anything to prop myself up in the world. I just needed to be the person whom God had already said I was. Being is so much easier—and so much more satisfying—than doing. I didn't chase the brass ring or the faux diamonds of earthly life. An exhausted man who had trudged through life, I finally rested. Through no striving of my own, I was presented with a treasure chest. When it was opened, I saw a cache of riches that were just for me. This treasure chest is offered to any who is open to receiving it.

The gems sparkled with divine color. The retina at the back of my spiritual eyes was awakened and received this fantastic display of riches. It bathed my soul in its splendor that I believe is one small crack of the colors of eternity. I became more intimately acquainted with the maker of light and color himself.

It was during this time when I bathed in this new found discovery of God's beauty and goodness that cancer reared its ugly head. Immediately, instinctively, like Pavlov's dog, all my old thinking rushed back in. I questioned: *Was my new understanding of grace only a mirage? Was I deluded by it? Was it a counterfeit? Was it wishful thinking? Was it self-deception? Was it a desperate attempt to gloss over once again?*

The twin voices of shame and condemnation roared back. Cancer was a death sentence. And I still wondered if really, deep down, I deserved it.

# "My sheep hear my voice"

John 10:27

# VOICE OF THE SHEPHERD

The Voice of life and truth came alive when Jesus came to earth.

The Bible even calls him "the Word." That Word is actually God himself. "In the beginning was the Word, the Word was with God, and the Word *was* God."

When he burst upon the earth, suddenly "the Word was made flesh and dwelt among us."

The Word that existed before time began—the expression that was there at creation when God breathed it into Adam and Eve—was now given full voice here among us.

What was breathed—then lost—was now found. All people could once again, through Christ, not only have unrestricted access to God's Voice, but that Voice—that Word—could live through them. It was no longer something out there. It was something within.

Jesus said, "My sheep hear my voice and I know them and they follow me." Jesus was not only restoring the communication between God and man, he was also restoring the idea of being known.

No longer would we need to hide ourselves from God, like Adam and Eve did in the garden, concealing our true selves. By following Christ, and listening to the Good Shepherd's Voice, we could come out of hiding. We could discover the maker of the universe in all his fullness and discover the person he intended us to be.

The Good Shepherd is calling... calling... calling.

We hear and follow what was, what can be, what is.

# CHAPTER 5

# THE *DOER*

I was about to become voiceless. A complete laryngectomy. But I wasn't going to go down without a fight. With my brother Terry's help, I set out on a quest to find someone—anyone—who might have an alternative treatment for my cancer.

Of course, Randy, the doer, got doing. In direct marketing we collect volumes of research to inform our decisions—to eliminate what doesn't work, so that we can zero in on what does. I applied that same approach to finding a cure. My brother and I spanned the globe researching which doctors might have an alternative to the terrible treatment and surgery that had been prescribed.

Also, at the agency, we create comprehensive, systematic plans specific to each client for the year. In a sense, I became both the client and the agency. I put together a thick, 3-ring binder of information, garnered from doctors and medical facilities from around the world. I contacted doctors in Sweden, Japan, and Spain, as well as Sloan Kettering in New York. All in all, I consulted with 27 doctors in four countries.

But my wide-ranging search to find that one solution was in vain. The doctors all said the same thing. I had to have that radical surgery or I would die.

Randy the doer couldn't work or plan his way out of this one. My extreme effort had come up short. I was at the mercy of this terrible problem. I couldn't control it. It controlled me. For a doer, that creates a multiplied sense of hopelessness. With each doctor contacted, and the same diagnosis and treatment confirmed, my despair grew.

Extra effort would not resolve this. It was unresolvable. My thick 3-ring binder was only a mocking testament to my hopeless plight. It didn't show what could be done. It spelled out, in great detail, what could not be done.

Thankfully, I had many people who lifted me up in prayer. In my helpless state, I actually began to be real. I couldn't just play it cool, or act like I was fine. I wasn't. I was inconsolably troubled. And no amount of posturing would solve it. The walls I built around myself had to be torn down. I had to embrace a radical new concept: vulnerability.

Humans try desperately to maintain control. We believe the weak can get trampled on and ultimately lose. But God offers true words of life: "…when I am weak, then I am strong" (2 Cor. 12:10). Herein is a great paradox. In God's economy, weakness is the pathway to power. Why? Because when we allow ourselves to let go, that's exactly when we find we aren't falling. Through God's power we're flying. In fact, the Bible says we can actually soar.

Letting go of human strength (or what we value as strength) is really powerful and wise. By definition, human strength is actually incredibly limited. Why hold on to something that is less when we can access something that is so much more?

There's a story about a little kid who got his hand stuck in a priceless vase. As much as everyone tried, they could not free him. His hand just wouldn't come out. They finally decided to smash the precious vase to free the child's hand. The vase cracked open, they discovered the child was making a fist. That's why his hand couldn't come back out through the narrow top of the vase. The exasperated parents asked the child, "Why didn't you just open your fist?" The child opened his hand and showed a marble. "I just didn't want to let go of it," he said.

We all clutch earthly things that at times actually destroy the priceless things right around us. We miss the mark of what's truly important.

This is what I discovered in the frightening moments after my long, fruitless search. It sounds strange now, but I feared that if I opened up, someone might not like me. I was concerned that if I was real I might get taken advantage of. But God himself did not let me succumb to my fears. With nowhere to turn, I opened up to sources of strength all around me.

I poured out my heart to a handful of dear friends. I came to know a young man named Jeudy (French for Tuesday, the day he was born). He was a leader in a Cambodian church, a non-profit leader in Compton, CA, and married to a wonderful young school teacher. He was simply there for me. He would read Scripture to me. He didn't offer earth-shattering pronouncements, but his kindness and presence were a great comfort.

In those harrowing moments, the simplest things had profound meaning and power. For instance, shortly after my diagnosis, I went to get some ice cream. As I walked down the driveway, I was startled by something in the shadows. At first I thought it was a cat. But then I saw clearly: it was a possum. While it's a harmless animal, it still caused me to turn around and head back into my house. A few minutes later, my doorbell rang. It was my friend Jeudy. He showed up unannounced with ice cream. If that possum hadn't been there, I would have left and missed him.

This might seem like a simple coincidence. But it is what I needed at that moment. It showed me a God who cares about the simplest details of my life. In my most desperate moments, I got calls from my worship pastor and friend, Darryl. "How are you doing?" was his simple question. And I would cry. Not just tears of anguish over my situation. I released years of holding back tears. It takes a tremendous amount of energy not to be your true self. You have to continuously monitor every word and action. You project a myth. And to keep that fable going requires extreme attention.

At this moment in my life, I asked why hold back? In the grander reality that was my life, why not just let go? I had nothing to lose. I was literally facing death, or a living death that was unfathomable to me. Why hide anymore? I wasn't that kid escaping to the space by the dryer. I was a man who needed to come out from his hiding and bare my soul. I couldn't conceal the real Randy any longer.

And wonder of wonders, my fears were destroyed. They were actually replaced by a love and an acceptance I had never known. My friends came to my rescue in my darkest hour. I didn't have to have it all together. I needed to express need, and that was not only okay, it was liberty incarnate. God used the sharp, harsh reality of a strangling cancer to allow me to breathe—to free the real person inside.

The desolation of spirit that I felt was assuaged by this host of comforters. My friends prayed for me, stood with me and encouraged me. The church elders and leaders anointed me with oil and prayed for me. Other friends prayed and interceded on my behalf. I think of the opening aria in Handel's "Messiah." The words are taken from the book of Isaiah, "Comfort ye, comfort ye my people" (Isa. 40:1 KJV). A great comfort came to me from God through other people. I was not just receiving from the outside, but feeling and experiencing from the inside a kindness I had never known.

Those blessed people were the anti-cancer. They weren't a pathology of cells seeking to destroy me. They were health and wholeness breathed into my spirit.

Despite the outpouring of love all around me, the bad news made it hard to believe that God was hearing any of our pleas. Yes, I had a new freedom—a new expression or authenticity. But with that also came the real concerns and fears. I expressed them as well. I wondered if heaven turned a deaf ear. How ironic. With the last bit of voice that I had, I was crying out to him. And it seemed like he wasn't listening.

There was a death rattle in my throat. But the Giver of Life seemed uninterested. At times, I was like Job wailing: *"Why? Where are you? What have I done to deserve this? You could change this, yet you don't."* One moment I was angry with him. In the next, I was completely undone, like a child yammering. At other times I was like the earnest, determined woman in the Bible who "...because of her importunity, the judge granted her request."

Frankly, I was a wreck. My psyche was in utter turmoil. Looking back, I realize that all—yes, *all*—of those emotions and appeals were okay. Growing up I was taught to believe that in times of trouble you might offend God if you raise your voice. Instead, we were told to just be quiet and behave. If you do ask him for things, keep your conduct in check. Be a super-performer not only before people, but before God.

I have come to realize that our earnest pleas are actual music to God. David wrote in the Psalms: "I pour out my complaint before Him; I declare my trouble before Him" (Ps. 142:2). God isn't like my earthly father, who would ignore me. God has ears that not only hear, but also welcome our voice.

Does my loud pleading offend him? Does he tune me out? Not at all. Why? Because he sees the earnestness of my heart. In other words, would I be crying out to him if I didn't believe that he would answer? Again, despite the cacophony coming forth, he sees who we really are. And he cherishes it. He doesn't care about the noise. He cares about the passion behind it. The trumpet of my humanness may be playing some blaring or out-of-tune notes, but I as the trumpet player filling the instrument with my very breath is—and wants to be—an integral part of the Lord's symphony.

Despite our collective pleas, it appeared God was not going to answer. It was incredibly discouraging and frightening.

Just when I was about to pull the trigger on the surgery and declare that his grace and power had failed me, I received a phone call: "Dr. Kokot would like to see you."

The doctor sat me down, drew a crude diagram and laid out a radical idea. He would attempt a surgery taking skin and blood vessels from my wrist and forearm, skin from my thigh and bone cartilage from my rib. He would fashion a new trachea from these spare parts. Yes, he would remove the cancer and with it much of my windpipe. But then, he would insert this newly manufactured, intricately fashioned replacement piece.

I knew this surgical maestro specialized in conservation surgery of the throat, which is designed to treat cancers of the larynx (voice box) without sacrificing speech or requiring permanent tracheostomy. But this all sounded a bit like science fiction. Skin from my forearm would become my new throat?

I couldn't help but be a bit cynical. "What success rate have you had?" I asked.

"Well, theoretically…" the surgeon said.

I wryly chuckled. I was to be Dr. Kokot's guinea pig. He was going to cut me open and patch me back together with baling wire and duct tape.

Dr. Kokot added, "It's worth a shot."

Then a little light glowed. Could it be? Could it possibly be that God had heard our pleas? Was the maker of the universe going to use this surgeon to remake my throat?

My brother Terry put it in perspective: "There's your miracle."

I remember walking out of the doctor's office. Of course, it's almost always sunny in Southern California. But for so many months, and wave after wave of disheartening news, my head had been down—heavy laden with the dire future before me. But now with this proposed surgery, it was as if the clouds of despair and heartache had indeed parted. I paused and looked up at that glorious sunshine. Perhaps the rays of hope were finally shining down.

The vulnerability—the weakness—that I had allowed was coming back with real power, real strength. For months I felt like a man on a sailboat who had sat on a windless ocean. With no wind to power the boat, I was stuck there, not able to move. I had desperately tried to row. But the ship wouldn't budge. Now a fresh, brisk wind began to blow—a zephyr of God's kindness. The sails of my life filled with a newfound energy. I moved forward. But it wasn't under my power. It wasn't because of Randy, the doer. That guy had been completely undone, and a new weak person, relying on God's strength, was emerging. It was his remarkable power that had magnificently intervened.

Standing there in the sunshine outside the doctor's office, I thought, *All I have to do is feel the possibility of the sun shining and experience the power of the wind as it moves me forward on a new course.*

## "Ephphatha!...
## Be opened!"

Mark 7:34

# Voice of Miracles and Healing

A miracle, by definition, is something that changes the course of the natural world. It turns sickness to healing, water to wine, hunger to feeding, death to life.

What releases that supernatural power into the natural realm? What is the portal that opens possibilities outside the limitations of our physical world?

Quite simply it is words. Or more specifically, "the Word" made alive.

Jesus didn't wave a magic wand. He didn't say incantations. And he certainly didn't prescribe some arduous course of sacrifice. No, when faced with disease and sickness, he simply spoke.

It was the same power and Voice that God himself used to speak the creation into existence. Jesus used words—or the very Voice of God—to reset the physical world to what it was initially: perfect, pristine and complete. It's like rebooting a malfunctioning computer operating system, restoring it to the original, uncorrupted version.

When confronting a deaf man who had a speech impediment, Jesus "...looked up to heaven and with a deep sigh said to him, 'Ephphatha! (which means 'Be opened!'). At this, the man's ears were opened, his tongue was loosened and he began to speak plainly" (Mark 7:34 NIV).

To open the man's ears, Jesus had to open the healing, restorative power of the universe. His exclamation, "Be opened!" was the word—the Voice—that unlocked the resounding power of eternity.

A Roman centurion came to Jesus because his servant was sick and dying. Jesus offered to go with the man and heal the servant. But the centurion knew Jesus didn't need to physically travel there. No, all he had to do was to speak: "But say the word, and my servant will be healed" (Luke 7:7 NIV). Jesus agreed, spoke and healed the man from a distance.

Words are power. Words spoken by and through the spirit tap "re"-creation power. And in so doing the things on this earth are transformed, made right and restored.

Jesus said, "If you abide in me, and my words abide in you, ask whatever you wish, and it will be done for you" (John 15:7).

# CHAPTER 6

# A MIRACLE SURGERY

---

O n the day of the surgery, my friend Jeff picked me up. We drove through the pre-dawn quiet to the USC Keck Hospital. Los Angeles—the massive, over-crowded metropolis—would wake up soon. As we drove, mostly in silence, down the freeway into this City of Angels, I could almost feel those spiritual guardians moving alongside me. Despite my underlying anxiety, I could sense a larger presence surrounding me.

I walked into the hospital feeling relatively fine. Other than the earache, I had the health of a twenty-something, as I had been told.

After they had prepped me, Dr. Kokot came in and said, in the matter-of-fact tone of a scientist, "If you wake up with a cast on your left arm, it means the surgery was successful." Of course, no cast meant no reconstructed throat. They would have removed the larynx.

Where were those angels now?

Pastor Scott had prayed for me saying, "You will not lose your voice. You have too much to say." But now in that cold hospital, my faith was waning. His words, while so powerfully assuring, began to fade under the sterile pre-op lights.

Imagine the anxiety going under anesthesia not knowing whether you'll wake up with a voice? But there was no turning back. My last memory was the white ceiling and lights of the operating room. They soon faded as I went into the darkness of anesthetized sleep.

When I woke up, I was anything but fine. In fact, I was a mess. The one who had the health of a twenty-something, now was in agonizing pain. I was trapped within a tangle of tubes, I.V's, and a catheter. I was sick from the anesthesia—hot, sweaty and in agony.

In my groggy state, I managed to look over. And there was a cast on my left arm! While good news, I was in no mood to celebrate. I couldn't even manage a smile. I was miserable. Not only was there a cast, there was an incision in my chest where they retrieved the rib cartilage and also a cut on my upper leg to secure a skin graft. The most excruciating misery, of course, was my throat. It throbbed. Worse, I could not speak at all. Not even a raspy squeak. I couldn't utter a word.

My assistant, Zack, was the first person to see me. He took one look and passed out! Other friends came to my bedside. Jeff had stayed the whole day through the surgery. Jeudy, my brother and Nancy were all there, too. They certainly tried to offer comfort. But the doctor had flayed me open and stitched me back up, and frankly, there was little that could alleviate my pain.

I was stuck behind ICU glass for four days. It was so horrific; I honestly thought it might have been better if I had just kept the cancer and that terrible earache until I died. They awoke me *every hour* to check the blood flow in my reconstructed throat. They said if the operation were a failure, it would be evident in the first seven days. The sleep interruption and deprivation took its toll, physically and emotionally. I came apart.

Worse, at night I heard workers waxing the floors. The drone of the machines drove me crazy. I complained—in writing, of course—to the nurses. In fact, I was anything but a model patient. God bless them for tolerating my written outbursts and demands. (Later, after I was back on my feet, I went back to the hospital and apologized for my terrible behavior.)

I was completely and utterly out of control. Like an infant, I couldn't even go to the bathroom on my own. Emotionally, it was like I was that six-year-old boy—helpless, trapped once more in a dysfunctional home. The adult Randy had worked so hard for years never to be in a helpless position again. But now I was pinned down and in physical misery.

But in those moments of utter powerlessness, my new friend, grace, found me—the real me. Grace had not abandoned me. She came forth with all her lavish goodness.

I listened to music. As I heard the sweet refrains about God's spirit and letting go, my spirit did just that. I let go of those last vestiges of control—the fear of losing control, really. Why hold on? What did I have to hold on to anyway? An extremely disruptive past? A compromised life? A meaningless life of distraction? A trumped-up sense of importance? Why hold on to any of that?

My weakness had been taken to the ultimate extreme. In my letting go, I received God's strength in new, unfathomable ways.

Not able to speak, I became the ultimate listener. In the 17th century, a simple monk named Brother Lawrence lived at a monastery in France. While he humbly did the most mundane tasks as a dishwasher and sandal repairer, he became aware of how to listen to God. He wrote a short but profound treatise called *Practicing the Presence of God*. One quote was particularly relevant, given my circumstances: "Stand there before God like a poor, mute paralytic at the door of a rich man."

That's exactly the position I was in. In essence I was a paralytic, bound to a hospital bed, unable to move. And in the first days after the surgery, I was mute. I couldn't utter a word. I had really no choice but to stand (or in my case, lay) before God. I was held before him, the rich man possessing all the treasures of the universe.

Confined to a hospital bed, bound by tubes and catheters and intravenous needles—with no physical voice—I found my inner soul crying out with a newfound abandon. I felt like I could stop struggling and let go. I could stop hanging on so tightly. I could stop fighting so hard to maintain that false self. After all, why was I protecting a counterfeit?

My friend Jeudy came, pulled out his online Bible and read Scripture. I had mentored Jeudy for ten years, and now he was ministering to me. The power of those words of life, coming from one of my comforters—or I should say, one of God's divine comforters—touched me to my core. Tears began to flow.

Jeudy asked why I was crying.

"I'm not sad," I said. "I'm just letting go."

It wasn't a one-time unburdening. Layers upon layers had built up over the years. My psyche was like an old house that had been painted over numerous times. Each layer of paint—or in my case whitewash—had to be stripped off. But unlike the arduous labor of stripping paint, this was not laborious at all. Just the opposite.

I didn't have a grueling task. Taking off a heavy load—like taking off a heavy backpack—is actually easy. You simply pull the straps off your aching shoulders and lay it down.

The tears, in part, were tears of joy. I was astounded by the simplicity of it all. The ease of God's goodness. Growing up, I was taught that any good thing from God had to be earned. I had to be a super-performer. Now, that misconception was met with an inner joy, even laughter, at my great good fortune.

I came to a place with God, through tears, where I was not just willing, but finally able to let go of this stranglehold of dysfunction that had been wrecking my life. Growing up, I wasn't allowed to express emotion through tears. Up to that point, I maybe had cried in public one time. But now the tears flowed freely. They didn't just run down my cheeks. They washed over my very being. They watered the drought-stricken desert that was my soul. The expression "like water to a thirsty man" took on new meaning. The Lord was offering his cup of goodness, and I drank with a joy and satisfaction I'd never known.

I was confined to a hospital bed, but my spirit was being liberated.

I cut—or rather I allowed the Lord to cut—the strings of the evil puppet-master that wanted to control me. I wasn't his marionette. I was no one's puppet. No, I was a human being, filled with an eternal pulse. I was a child of God, experiencing the same breath that God had first breathed into Adam—the breath of life.

Real tears rolled down my cheeks. This was true, human expression coming out, perhaps for the first time. David cried out when he was hiding in a cave from Saul, who wanted to kill him, "You have taken account of my wanderings; Put my tears in your bottle. Are they not in your book? This I know, that God is for me. For you have delivered my soul from death. So that I may walk before God in the light of the living" (Ps. 56:8-13).

Grace had waited patiently, keeping my tears that were hidden even from me. God knew the pain they represented. He kept them. But now he allowed me to release them. The bottle of true tears was being poured out. He delivered me not only from physical death, but also from the fatality of belief in my false self. The murder of an innocent was now being rectified and restored. And with each salty teardrop, I felt life emerging from the inside out like I had never known.

As I lay in the hospital, I was finally quiet, still and out of control enough to hear God. Perhaps I heard his Voice because I couldn't hear my own—for once. In my silence, I was open to that wonderful Voice from eternity, calling, speaking and filling me with words of truth and comfort. The amazing thing about God speaking to us is not just the message in those words, but the fact that we know he actually is speaking. The God of the universe is whispering to us individually, like an intimate friend, like a gracious father, like something that was always meant to be. His Voice was now animating and filling a great void within me.

The interplay of the Spirit of an all-encompassing God divinely speaking to and through us is a great mystery. This is not something anyone can easily define in human terms. But as it happens, it actually isn't something odd. In fact, one of the hallmarks is that it feels entirely, completely normal. It's as if we are stereo speakers and have been waiting for music to finally play through us. God's Voice through us is completely the way we were designed and utterly what he intended all along.

As I cried, I released the years of resistance to that sweet refrain pulsing through me. I heard God. And those first utterances through me were indescribable joy! "Randy, I AM THAT I AM is here." Moses had heard God refer to himself in the burning bush. And now I heard that same Voice from eternity.

# "...whom Jesus loved"

John 13:23

# VOICE OF INTIMACY

He heard the Lord's heartbeat.

John was so close to Jesus that he laid his head on his chest.

And what did he hear?

Within, between and among those gentle rhythms, love was being transmitted from the Lord's heart to his own. For John described himself as the disciple "whom Jesus loved."

This wasn't some personal favoritism. No, he was simply asserting something that is true for all who believe.

He was hearing what the prophet Elijah described as "a still small voice."

God's Voice, at times, comes to us in a whisper. Why? Because as David wrote, "Your gentleness makes me great."

This is intimacy at its finest. An almighty, all-knowing, all-powerful God is not some distant reality. No, he comes like Jesus said as a dear friend: "No longer do I call you slaves, for the slave does not know what his master is doing; but I have called you friends, for all things that I have heard from My Father I have made known to you" (John 15:15).

Jesus heard the heartbeat of God. And he wants to make that very pulse known to each of us. Indeed, as we listen, we discover that our entire being begins to move to the gentle rhythms of God, not only weaving in and through us, but out to other people who often think God is harsh and distant.

Jesus hears the heartbeat of the universe.

He offers it to us.

And we give it to the world.

# CHAPTER 7

# REST

I now had a throat of spare parts. It was remanufactured by the skilled hands of a wonderful surgeon.

At first, I couldn't talk. But then after a few days, they did a small procedure—the slightest adjustment to my throat—and my physical voice was back. I could speak!

No more trying to scribble words on a pad. And certainly no more fear that somehow the doctor had screwed up and I would be left voiceless. Audible sounds and words flowed. Randy, the communicator, could once again communicate.

It was still a painful recovery. I had a temporary tracheotomy or hole in my throat that allowed me to breathe. But this required regular cleaning. In fact, they would insert a tube down into the lung cavity and turn on what amounted to a vacuum cleaner, sucking out any fluid that might lead to an infection. It was like getting electrocuted; they did this four or five times a day.

The first time they got me up to walk, I nearly passed out. They said I had to be able to walk up the stairs before I could be released from the hospital. Initially, that was impossible. In those first few days, even the act of taking a few vertical steps caused my heart rate to shoot up.

But slowly, day by day, I recovered and regained my physical strength. I was eventually discharged and went home to recover.

Over the next several days and weeks, the healing continued. Not only was the cancer in my throat gone, the spiritual cancer that had wrecked my soul was also being radically removed. I had a new—albeit refashioned—throat. In many ways, the physical surgery was secondary to the deeper operation. The Creator's work was not made of existing parts. No, there was a reboot, a fresh life, a new creation birthed within. Theologically, I knew that it had been there all along. So technically, I was just waking up to what "was and is and is to come."

I had been saved since I was a pre-teen. The Lord had come into my life. But this second or expanded act of grace was in itself a rebirth. Seeds that had been dormant for years sprang up into new growth.

God moved in simple but profound ways. I had been literally opened up physically by a surgeon. But also, throughout this process, the rigid defenses that I had so adamantly held in place got flayed open as well. It was a soul exposed.

When I was initially diagnosed, I posted on social media what I was facing. Within a few minutes, Daryl, the worship pastor, called me. He only said, "How are you?" And I came unglued. Here again was another comforter. Again, no great declarations. Just a transformed person, being there for another.

My pastor, Scott, was another comforter. He stood with me throughout. He boldly said, "We're not praying that you would be healed. We're praying that you are already healed. You will not lose your voice," he said emphatically. He quoted the Scripture, "No weapon formed against you will prosper," and added, "Where you may be waffling, I am an advocate." He was, in essence, a bulwark for my tormented spirit.

After the surgery, God used other people as well. Throughout my life, the opportunity to find resonance had been cut off. As a child, a pattern was ingrained that simple exploration of who I was as a unique person was not only discouraged, it was outright dismissed. So I stuffed that impulse. But now my voice, my emotions, spilled out and through these new sounding boards, the truth and substance of something greater came back.

Rest, after all, is just that: not giving up but offering up all that is troubling you. It's his problem. Not mine.

This is what God offers to all people. No matter your burden. Jesus said, "Come to Me, all who are weary and heavy-laden, and I will give you rest" (Matt 11:28). I suppose if you don't feel weak and you don't carry heavy burdens, then that Scripture is not for you. But I know we all have something we're carrying around. I can only hope yours isn't the same as my stifling experience when I was growing up. But each has that weight they must bear.

I can't help but encourage each of you reading these words to discover the true joy of simply letting it go. The God of the universe is not only there ready to catch it and take it for you as you "cast all your cares on Him," He's also longing to reveal to you the true nature of himself, uniquely expressed through you.

I believe that when we rest, we are our true persona. We're suspended, if you will, by and through his power. Sometimes the storms still rage around us, but we have moved to the eye of the storm. When we are battered by life's problems, it seems counter-intuitive to move further into the storm. Our natural response is to move away as fast as we can. Then we face the danger of the fierce storms.

But God has another way. We move to the very place where he is— the very center of the storm. Everything may be whirling around us, but we're safe. Rest is simply finding that sanctuary. The storm will— as will the problems we face—eventually break apart and dissipate. Calm, clear skies will once again prevail. We've arrived, unscathed, held by his rest.

# "...the stone...
# taken away
# from the tomb"

John 20:1

# VOICE OF SILENCE

On the cross, Jesus spoke seven last words that ring throughout eternity.

*Father, forgive them, for they know not what they do.*
*Today you will be with me in paradise.*
*Behold your son: behold your mother.*
*My God, my God, why have you forsaken me?*
*I thirst.*
*It is finished.*
*Father, into your hands I commit my spirit.*

However, there was an even greater voice that came three days later.
It was the voice of silence.
An empty tomb.
Death had been defeated. Death could not speak. Death now had no voice.
All the clamor of a world filled with heartache, anguish, evil and self-interest was nullified—rendered speechless.
The voice that harkened back to the corruption in the garden was finally crushed.
In that pristine moment of silence, all the power of goodness, joy and love emerged.
A hush did proceed from this empty tomb that still offers a clear call for us today. It invites all people to let go of the toxic clamor in their own lives and enter into that place of perfect peace, where the very whispers of God can be heard.
Yes, a dying man cried out on a cross.
However, his death was a crushing annihilation of evil. For in its place came a hope that we each could find that reborn silence prepared for all who would believe.

# CHAPTER 8

# YOU SWALLOWED YOUR WORDS

Fresh revelations and newfound freedoms kept coming to me, even as I faced an arduous rehabilitation. I went through occupational, physical, and speech therapy. I even had to have swallow therapy and learn how to perform the most mundane tasks of eating and drinking again.

The larger treatment plan didn't end with just the surgery. Cancer is an insidious pathology. If you don't get rid of every last cell, it can rear its ugly head again. So Phase II of my treatment plan was intense radiation. As the doctors described these treatments, a new round of fear was stirred up.

They were about to bombard my throat with a focused laser. And not just a few times. No, I had to endure 33 rounds—with one treatment every day. While there was no physical cutting, there would be a powerful, concentrated beam of energy so strong it could destroy flesh. In fact, they fitted me with a custom facemask that protected everything but my throat from the radiation.

Even with the mask in place, there was potentially horrible, collateral damage. The doctor listed a litany of possible outcomes. I could lose teeth, lose taste buds and the ability to taste altogether, lose the ability to salivate, permanently, lose all appetite, and end up cutting weight to dangerously low levels.

I was about to go under a laser. (I pictured some horrific torture chamber James Bond might find himself in). Again, the word *loss* rang deep down inside, terrorizing me. The losses I had no control over. I was at their mercy.

However, I had a new counter-attack to that fear. It was called grace—not being led by my fears but being swept up in the Spirit. I wasn't at the mercy of fear; I was caught up in the mercies of God.

To bolster my emotional and spiritual position, I had an amazing new weapon: music. As mentioned I had always been drawn to music, performing as a young man and promoting bands as an adult. But now music was so much more than either pursuit. I wasn't just playing or promoting music, I was living it. The melodies of heaven were bathing me in not just their truth, but in their power.

The Bible says, we "offer up a sacrifice of praise…" (Heb. 13:15). Praise or music is indeed a sacrifice. That seems odd at first glance. But with an expanded understanding, I came to realize that music was a portal to freedom. It's a reminder to the soul to let go. Like praise, music beacons us to sacrifice: to raise the white flag of surrender. But that surrender is not some milquetoast cowardice. No, it is a deliberate unburdening. It is admitting and embracing your own human weakness and willfully laying it down, sacrificing it on the altar.

In praise, people will often lift their hands. That can be intimidating. Why? Because it is a physical display of vulnerability.

Raising your hands isn't to show someone else that you are humble. It is an outward expression of an inward humility and release. (I've often found it curious that even at secular rock concerts people freely and unabashedly raise their hands. God designed music to have the power, whether conscious or not, to set people free.)

Music is an integral part of letting go. Of course, listening to music doesn't always cause oneself to raise their physical hands. But music can free oneself on the inside. It is an inner liberation, or rather a springboard to freedom.

As I walked into that hospital and received my radiation treatments for 33 days in a row, I brought my music. They let me blast it as I lay under the radiation laser each day. I brought a sacrifice of praise to my inner man. I laid down my fears on his altar. I knew that the burning up of them was not only a sweet aroma to God, but also unto myself. In fact, you could say there is nothing more sweet than to burn up destructive fear and anxiety, to destroy the shackles that bind, to raze self-condemnation. That is what music allowed me to do.

As these terrible oppressions were extinguished, they were replaced by unexpected joys. After all, music beyond being a sacrifice is a life-giving concerto of joy. It reaches and touches places in the soul that can't be touched by mere human logic or willpower. In other words, I couldn't just tell myself, "You'll be okay … you'll be okay." No, I had to feel and know that I would not only be okay, but I would rise above. The transcendence of music leads us to that higher place.

My new attitude began to spill out. I made friends, got to know and spend time with the doctors, nurses and technicians in a way that made the time almost fun. I brought in a big gift basket. Instead of approaching radiation as a doomsday event, I began to speak with that Voice that had spoken to me and was now speaking out through me. The waiting room at a radiation center is filled with people in bad shape. I not only refused to succumb to being in bad shape, but I tried to be an encouragement to those hurting people.

On each of those 33 days, it wasn't Randy "the doer" who walked into that hospital. Rather, I became Randy "the drummer-musician in the Lord's symphony." Randy "the-releaser-of-self." Randy "the-praise-maker." Randy "the-receiver-of-divine-goodness." Randy "the-conduit-of-grace."

Lo and behold, the dire possible outcomes from the radiation that the doctors had described did not occur. Did I lose teeth? No. Lose taste buds? No. Lose saliva? No. Lose weight? No. In fact, on my new diet of milkshakes (prescribed because my throat was raw), I gained 19 lbs! The doctor actually had to tell me, "You can stop eating now."

In the midst of this process, I met with an Asian friend who studies and practices Chinese medicine. Beyond the physical analysis, he offered another interesting perspective. He told me that there were hidden implications given that this particular disease had showed up in my throat. From his Eastern perspective, he offered this broader insight: "You swallowed your words," he said.

I'm not superstitious. And I don't think there's a retribution—or bad karma—for bad actions taken. Obviously, when we make poor choices, we suffer consequences. But my friend's thought offered meaning for me. It was a profound picture of what had happened. The fact is, I had been swallowing my words my entire life. I had stuffed them, or rather, the situation I grew up in would not allow them to come out.

But the wonderful thing about how God moves is this: he calls himself the Word. But this label does not refer to dry, dictionary terms. No, he is a living Word. So despite all the forces conspiring to have me swallow my words, the true Word, the living Word within me would not be denied its expression. Because it—or rather he residing within me—is a living Word. No earthly dead thing can keep the living Word from coming forth.

Yes, I had swallowed my words. But in God's great sovereignty and abounding love, he transformed those suppressed words, and I discovered new words that were actual nourishment and even nurture. They came out, expressing themselves with the abundant richness that had always been at their core.

The Bible says that God's word "will not return unto me void." What that meant in my life was, the living Word that had been implanted within me from my childhood was indeed not going to lay dormant or somehow just fade away. No, it has a divine energy within it that will not be denied. The author of the Word is the author of the universe. He is not going to rest until that Word is fully expressed. He will use all means necessary to make it come alive. Oh, I might swallow my earthly words, but his heavenly Word will still be expressed.

Initially, I thought cancer was a punishment. Ironically—and this is the nature of how God works—the new thing I was learning was suddenly juxtaposed against a horrible thing. But it is the nature of God to allow this counterpoint. We see the light the most clearly in a dark room. It's hard to see gray against gray or even light in the middle of light. You can't see a car's lights that well during the day, but you can see them coming a mile away at night.

I came to realize with even more fervor and clarity the truth of Romans 8:28: "And we know that all things work together for good..." God was turning even the darkness of cancer into a new understanding of his glorious light. From my experience, not all the things that happen in this life are good. But God promises to take even the worst possible things and turn them for good in the life of the believer. In my case, swallowed words were becoming the expressed Word of Life, in and through me. Good abounded, despite the terrible scourge of cancer. The Voice, so squelched, was finding a new, vibrant articulation.

The Bible says, "It is for freedom that Christ has set us free" (Gal. 5:1 NIV). I was experiencing this freedom in fantastic, new ways. The words I had swallowed were no longer sequestered. The living Word was now free to come out. The cancer that would have produced the death of me was, through God's grace, fostering life. This horrible, inhuman experience that no one should have to go through, unleashed an altogether lovely human within me.

Swallowed and sequestered became released and reborn!

# "a...rushing wind"

Acts 2:2

## VOICE OF THE WIND

The disciples waited.

Jesus had promised them that they would receive power. They would be baptized not with water but with the Spirit.

And then, a sudden sound.

"...there came from heaven a noise like a violent, rushing wind, and it filled the whole house where they were sitting."

God spoke yet again. This time with a fresh, bold voice.

The wind was a disruption, blowing away the old. More importantly, it was ushering in the new. It filled them with a radical power and purpose.

The Spirit was as potent as flames of fire. But these weren't flames that consumed, but rather an eternal fuel that drove them from within.

With this Spirit came not only the fruit and attributes of God: patience, truth, endurance, gentleness and compassion. The Spirit also brought the amazing gifts of evangelism, healing, prophecy, supernatural wisdom and restoration of the poor and needy.

The Living Word had come alive within them. A new kingdom was birthed. But this wasn't in the political or national domain. No, this kingdom did "...not consist in words but in power."

Like the apostles, we have access to this same Spirit. We can receive not just attributes and gifting, but our core spirit is transformed, "For in him we live, and move, and have our being" (Acts 17:28).

We become a magnified version of ourselves.

We feel that rushing, internal wind.

We allow ourselves to experience the beauty of being blown off the normal course of our limitations.

We are transported to an entirely expanded world that purifies and quickens us with a vibrant, new vision.

# CHAPTER 9

# A NEW SONG

During recovery, I continued to listen to music with more passion. These inspirational refrains took on new meaning. The choruses of truth and life continued to grow within me.

Some of the songs were just simple praise songs like "More Than Enough" and "Healer." But these songs opened a floodgate to expanded realities.

The Bible refers to a new song: "Sing to the Lord a new song; sing to the Lord, all the earth" (Ps. 96:1). This is far more than a tune played or sung. It is a transference. The old, out-of-tune, out-of-rhythm songs that had been imprinted on me since my youth were actually silenced. A new song came bursting forth. I heard, felt and lived new melodies—indeed symphonies—of love, acceptance, freedom and purpose.

I had been shamed into speechlessness. You could say nearly "cancered" into having no voice. Now I was learning to speak up. I was discovering that I was a unique song in the world. But now, as this awakening was occurring, I could say with honesty and not arrogance, "I have needs." "I'm disappointed." Or, "I'm afraid." I didn't try to cover it over. I was learning to be honest about my feelings. I leaned on God and others.

God was playing the instrument called Randy that he had always intended Randy to be. It was amazing to watch—or rather listen—to this new song. The funny thing was the new song, while fresh and alive, also felt like something ancient and altogether a part of who I was, always had been, and always will be. It was "me"—fearfully and wonderfully made. It was Randy created uniquely in the image of God, since before time began. I was an expression, an unfettered articulation. My voice rang not just within this physical world, but stretched back to the very foundational purposes of God. And that unique utterance that resounded within me extended forward to all eternity.

This understanding is hard even to put into words. But it resonated within me. I truly was a song—a voice ringing not just within the time span of years that I would have on this earth, but unlimited, unbounded and infinitely expanding throughout the universe of God's making.

I found it amazing that those thoughts came to me as I listened to melodies of praise. This was beyond mere music I was hearing. This rose above simple tones and rhythms. This was the Maker of Music himself playing Randy as an instrument of purpose and praise. I was designed and created for this by him. And now I was being played by him, the master musician. The true Randy was not only made by Stradivarius, I was being played by Itzhak Perlman. Those notes and discordant tunes I had tried to play for so many years on my own were altogether paltry, pathetic and lacking. They now were anathema to me.

I was a voice resounding from the center of my heart.

The chorus expanded further by my support network. It started slowly at first, when I was diagnosed. I let a few people know what was happening. But this group grew to over 100 people all over the world.

When I went in for surgery, my brother Terry became the point person. He updated my PR colleague and friend Mike Shepherd, who then updated my growing email group.

This correspondence was everything from short missives like, "Operation was successful" to "Stay away. Randy's having a bad day." Of course, we also updated my circle with more details about the specifics of the operations and procedures.

This communication became more than just simple, perfunctory news of the day. I became more vulnerable. It was okay to share not just the good, but also the bad and the ugly too. No whitewashing. I put that old paint bucket away.

This was Randy being real. Before I had worked so hard to conceal; now I was emancipated. It was so freeing. It made me wonder why I had kept everything sequestered for so long.

It was astonishing to have so many living sounding boards taking in my new expressions—then in turn, giving back their own encouragements. Friends locally and from around the world would write:

> "As I prayed to God in how thankful I've been for you in my life, I broke down in tears through the prayer. I stand firm that God has you in his arms and that he loves you until eternity. But want to encourage you that you've made a tremendous impact in my life and many others."

> "I am so happy that you are looking cancer in the face and saying it's not going to own you. God definitely has a plan for you."

> "The *whys* may not be answered in this life, but the *hows* are what magnify the power of Jesus. You are doing that now."

"You push me to reach new heights and to set the bar higher."

"Your amazing recovery reminds me of the constant hope and effort we must motivate ourselves on a daily basis and the brevity of life itself."

"You have such a positive attitude which cheers me up so much."

"We have had a great time praying for you. We sensed the Spirit of the Lord God at work in us and in your life."

"Praise God that in Him we can certainly be at peace and at rest regardless of our circumstances. Like you said, (or rather, Paul wrote in Romans), he works all things for good for his people. We can be certain of that!"

These exchanges were so refreshing. The human interaction and care that was short-circuited in my youth was restored. These people were more than the canyon walls echoing back to me. Each of them spoke new variations of truth.

It's a lot of work to keep a true person bottled up inside. I had to constantly check myself, making sure the image of Randy that I projected to the world remained intact. But now I expressed a true living, breathing person—a soul, made in the image of God who will live forever. How could anything temporary, or earthbound, restrain that being? It would be like a beaver thinking it could build a dam to hold back Niagara Falls, or a sailboat trying to direct the wind, rather than letting the wind direct it.

Now there was no false image. There was no cross-checking. There was just honesty, and this simple release of the truth did indeed set me free. I knew the reality down inside and part of that knowing is to let that genuineness be known by others.

As we know, communication is a two-way street, and I was now opening up one side—my side—of the freeway that I had blocked.

Not only was my support group simply sharing words of support, they also stepped up to help me. My dear friend, Phil Stolberg, actually took several weeks of vacation from another company to come in and manage Brewer Direct while I was out. Jeff not only sat in the waiting room, he also helped with many logistical challenges. Others continued to come over and just read scripture to me. My brother, Terry, continued to stand like a traffic cop, protecting me and also allowing information to flow. My assistant, Zack, stayed at my house for two weeks and helped with logistics. Of course, the people at my church continued to pray for me, including Pastor Scott and his staff. Rea Barnes would pray and send encouraging text messages throughout the day.

I was taught growing up to be a rock (don't cry) and an island (isolate and feel no pain). How opposite this is from the way God lives and moves. We are all part of the body of Christ, and each brings strength and support to the other members. To shut down and shut off is to deny oneself the rich tributaries of blessing that come from so many different sources.

I "sang a new song" to my chorus of support, and they in turn sang back. This is the nature of true relationship in God's symphony. All the musicians play off each other in the most amazing harmonies.

Perhaps the greatest support came from the most unexpected place. When I first learned of my cancer, I was understandably reticent to mention anything to my clients. My first impulse was to think that if they knew, they might leave the agency, fearing that in a diminished physical capacity, I would not be able to help them with their fundraising and marketing needs.

Nothing could be farther from the truth. Near the beginning of my ordeal, I spoke to one of my first Brewer Direct clients, Rick Alvis, at the Wheeler Mission in Indianapolis. I hadn't mentioned a word about my diagnosis. In some ways, I felt like I was lying by not saying anything.

Then out of the blue, he asked, "Is something wrong?" He could tell. We had been working together for ten or more years by then and—well—he just knew.

I told him the whole story. I have to admit, for the slightest moment, I didn't know how he would react. But then the most wonderful thing happened. Our relationship went beyond any business or fundraising considerations. Rick was there for me like a Christian brother. From across the country came the most heartfelt support, encouragement and, yes, love. I could only think of what people in other pure business relationships must encounter when these things arise. To hear Rick's simple words, "We'll be praying for you," meant everything.

As I began to let go of my own fears, I opened up about my illness with other Mission leaders. Without fail, they all reacted the same way. They put aside any concerns about our ability to service them as clients, and they got into the trenches with me. They were an outpouring of care and reassurance. They stood in the gap for me as true intercessors. The Mission became more than clients. They were a unique and unexpected support network.

A stream of emails, cards, gifts, and flowers began to flow in. Notes would come to me signed by the entire staff at a Mission. They believed with me and for me. I realized over and over again the true heart of these precious people. They weren't just committed to rescuing homeless people. They turned that same love and attention my way and rescued me.

## "Go into all the world…"

Mark 16:15

# VOICE TO THE WORLD

The world cries out for truth and peace. Often, it doesn't appear to be possible. Darkness is all around. Bitterness and hatred seem to be winning.

In spite of this, Jesus called us to be light-bearers. Candles shining in the dark. Voices of love and hope, going out to all the world.

There are hearts prepared not just to listen, but to truly hear.

In the world of sound, a pure tone can be cancelled out if the exact opposite sound wave is expressed at the same time. This is the experience for many in the world. They are a potential, living pure tone. But an opposite wave cancels them out. That opposite wave is a noise that harkens back to the fall in the garden; and now each person carries sin and death's marker even as they are born into this world.

People sense that they possess a potential pure tone. But this opposite noise blocks it.

As we share God's truth—the news about the one who conquered sin and death—that opposite tone is destroyed. The pure tone is released.

This expression of the Gospel's Voice has this effect: it is able to liberate each individual to their own uniqueness. The clamor that is constraining them—and would ultimately destroy them—is switched off. Without that uproar, the pure Voice is set free.

The most remarkable thing is this: sharing one's unique voice is the best way to release someone else's distinctive voice. Why? Because our unique voices are truth and light. Truth speaks to the truth within another.

We can rest in being ourselves in the world. Never underestimate or shy away from authenticity—your own voice. Others will hear it and by it may discover their own pure tone.

# CHAPTER 10

# RELEASING THE VOICES OF OTHERS

C ancer survivors can become "yes people." I suddenly found myself saying yes to so many opportunities to help less-fortunate people. The circle of connectivity began to increase exponentially.

This new expansion started with a simple question. Shannon, a friend and advisor, asked me: "What do you want to do?"

The answer was actually straightforward as well: "I want to help people around the world. I want to make a difference." But it was deeper than just doing good works. Gone was Randy the super-performer who felt under compulsion to act in counterfeit ways. Now, I wanted to live out the reality that had come alive within me. I wanted to share the genuine life testimony of how I came to understand this new life. I had a newly refashioned throat. With it came a reconstructed outlook.

It kicked off in October of 2012. I had a cancer-free celebration. After the surgery, then 33 rounds of radiation, my doctor declared me cancer-free. I thought we'd have a little party with a few of my friends. When I came in the house, I was shocked by how many people were there. It was packed. My little party was a grand celebration of not just my successful surgery, but it was an outpouring of unabashed love and support. I was overwhelmed. My friends all wore red—cancer-free—ribbons. They had propped me up and seen me through this ordeal, and now were ready to celebrate the victory.

Shortly after this, seemingly out of the blue, I began to receive invitations to go to places around the world. Actually, I don't believe these were mere happenstance. The Great Choreographer of truth and light arranged these invites. I began a cancer-free tour with stops first in Japan. Another surprisingly large, support group met me there. Next it was Thailand, Singapore, Indonesia and China.

I served on the board of a group called African Enterprise. In that capacity I had been an advisor, friend and supporter. Now I was asked by a board member to engage with the work in the field. Suddenly, I found myself on a trek to Rwanda and Kenya. As with most developing nation travel, I was staying in hotels with limited services. I bounced over dusty, rough roads to various outposts and villages. The physical accommodations were challenging. But I experienced God's spirit powerfully move in the most primitive settings. The world may have all but forgotten these places, but God certainly hadn't.

I heard the most fervent worship teams. This was another musical course within the lavish feast that God had offered to me through music. We imagine choirs of angels, perhaps coming down Jacob's ladder. But now I experienced this with full voice. These precious people echoed the choirs of heaven. The fresh, pure expressions were an unfettered conduit to the divine.

How interesting—and perhaps even tragic—that in the West we often put so many stops or mufflers on God's Voice. I suppose you could say we overthink it. The mind or so-called rational thought takes precedence over the move of the Spirit. This echoes the Scripture that says, "Professing to be wise, they became fools..." (Rom. 1:22).

However, here in this far-off place, the people were acutely open to the nearness of God. The curtain separating the earthly and the eternal was opened with unfettered, unabashed resolve. And why shouldn't it be? After all, the Bible says, "Man shall not live on bread alone, but on every word that proceeds out of the mouth of God" (Matt. 4:4). These unassuming people, through their praise and worship, heard and spoke and sang those very Spirit-sent words. And it was life to them and to me.

Randy the "yes man" had said no to his handcuffed and incarcerated life. And now with those prison doors flung open, I found myself walking out to a chorus of heaven's troubadours.

I met many families in Africa. I visited an orphanage called ByGrace Children's Home. The hardships they live under are overwhelming. So I became a child sponsor, helping several children with their daily and monthly needs.

After Africa, it wasn't long until I was back on another trans-oceanic flight. This time I headed west to Indonesia. Again, a divine arrangement was made. I jokingly call God the great travel agent, because who could plan such trips except him?

In this country, which is predominantly Muslim, I was swept up in the move of God's spirit. The Lord not only provided entre to speak to and help individual families, but also to speak over the airwaves to a larger audience.

At the invitation of World Harvest, I met a family with two children. One has Down Syndrome. I offered to take them out to eat at any restaurant. They chose KFC. I discovered that they could never afford even fast-food. What a simple joy to sit down with this under-privileged, unpretentious family who felt honored and excited to be eating fried chicken. How humbling for me.

The father only makes $150 a month. He pays $35 per month for a two-room shack the size of my office. Given their near penniless exis-tence, I was able to open a savings account ($100) for their children that will one day help them go to college. (Secondary school in Indonesia is so much less expensive than here in the States. So this amount—which I'm adding to over time—while miniscule to us, will actually provide the necessary funds one day for them to advance their education.)

In Indonesia I was also invited to be on *Good News* television. A Christian outreach interviewed me and allowed me to tell my story, broadcast it across the Indonesian airwaves. I'm not sure this was "shouting it from the mountaintops," but it was shouted via TV transponders. May the Lord use it to those unseen who hear not Randy, but the power of God through Randy.

The yeses continued. My spirit compelled me to help—to share. It was as if a new engine had been placed within me. I had a relentless fervor to reach out to any and all whom God placed in my path. I didn't—and still don't—say no. I truly follow every stream. The Bible says, "Let your gentle spirit be known to all men. The Lord is near" (Phil. 4:5). The Word also encourages us to be "…ready to make a defense to everyone who asks you to give an account for the hope that is in you, yet with gentleness and reverence" (I Pet. 3:15).

As I travel I look for opportunities where God is opening doors. I want to share how I was transformed by my experience of discovering my voice. I want to help others discover theirs, or rather, just listen to their voice. I find that the simple act of listening to them, helps them discover the enduring truths in their own lives. I am always looking for that opportunity.

Cancer humanized me. It has made me real. I realize I am less than super-human. It's made me more open and honest. I needed to be loved and touched. I am a rock, but for most of my life, I had set myself up as an island. Now I know I need to rely more and more on people.

The irony and wonderful benefit of this newfound openness is that as I open up, others open up to me. Sharing my freedom is freeing to them. And there is no greater joy than witnessing, even participating in, this liberation of another human being.

My new faith adventure of being sensitive to and following the leading of God's spirit has launched many vibrant pathways to others. I've never been married, and I have no wife or children of my own—no photographs of cute kids. But through God's divine grace, I have family and children all over the world. Here are just some of the wonderful people that God has brought across my path. These are rich, divine encounters, indeed:

## MJ in China

Following the Lord's leading (or I could say, just being God's "yes man" after my surgery), I ended up in China. I'm a huge Los Angeles Lakers fan, and I had an opportunity to see them play a preseason game in Shanghai.

I got to the arena an hour early, and so I looked around for a restaurant to grab something to eat. I only ordered a shake—a bit of cool refreshment on my new throat. Sitting there, I struck up a conversation with my waiter. I shared my story. The man, who goes by the name MJ, stood there for an hour, captivated by my ordeal.

We exchanged emails. He graciously began tracking and supporting my progress, along with my other group of wonderful friends. He was responsive, even as the emails became more Christian, as I shared the Gospel and addressed issues of faith. We started having separate conversations via live chat.

MJ got married and had a baby. But the baby became jaundiced. I told him that I would believe that God would heal their baby. I simply encouraged him that God was in charge. He ended the conversation by saying, "I believe God is in charge too." I sensed MJ coming to an understanding of faith and growing in it.

Coincidence? I don't believe so. I see God's hand moving in and through this entire divine encounter. If it had not been for cancer, I would not have been in China. Even that horrific negative—through God's grace—was turned into a positive. Arriving at the Lakers game early and meeting MJ wasn't random. God orchestrated something as simple as being ahead of schedule and the need to grab a bite to eat. I would even say that I wasn't there in that restaurant to order a shake. I was there as a part of God's plan to shake up the steps of MJ's life—to open his mind and heart to the larger workings of a loving God. Of course, I responded to the gentle nudging to strike up a conversation. But even this impulse, I attribute to God releasing me from my inhibitions. He had revealed to me—again through the scourge of cancer—a great healing and release of my true inner voice. That voice is what came through in that initial meeting and all the subsequent exchanges with MJ.

**Arin and Meg from Iran**

I call this a carwash encounter. I take my car to a certain carwash near my home. Arin, one of the managers, is from Iran. We struck up a conversation while my car went through the scrubbers. Of course, Arin couldn't help but notice, after my surgery, the bandages and cast. This immediately took our small talk to another dimension. He asked about me and my situation, which naturally led to me asking about his.

He told me about his struggle to make it in the U.S. His wife, Meg, was studying to become a nurse and working long hours at Macy's. They both missed their families and friends back in Iran. They are Christian by culture and of course would face much oppression if they had stayed in Iran.

I listened to his ordeal, desires and goals. I offered a Christmas bonus (a few extra bucks) and even took Arin and his wife to dinner one night where I learned much about their culture. And I shared my story.

We still stay in touch through texts and emails. But again, I don't see this as just another ordinary encounter. I certainly appreciate their friendship. After all, they reached out with compassion to me as I recuperated from my illness. But in the broader scope of life— this life and the one to come—I trust that I can be a transponder of God's Voice. When you listen to the radio, sometimes you have to adjust the dial to have the station come in more clearly. To me, this is what happens with so many on their journey of life. God is speaking, indeed sending out his music for the world to hear. But sometimes people need us to come alongside and adjust the tuner in their life a little so they can hear the broadcast.

## Chris, John, Alex, Peter and Others from ByGrace

In my journeys here and abroad, I always seem to run into young people. After I've gotten to know them a little better, again I can't help but play the role of mentor. I share *Randy's Three Rules of Success*: 1) Do what you say you'll do; 2) Be where you say you'll be; and 3) Be on time. A bonus rule is: If you want to be rich, be generous. These may seem extremely simple. But I've noticed that in many developing nation countries, and even here in the U.S., countless young people weren't even taught the fundamentals of human interaction. They simply don't know what to do or how to act in order to open doorways to expanded relationships—especially in a professional capacity. These rudimentary precepts resonate, though. And I find that these kids not only want to learn them, but desperately want to get ahead in life. The Bible asks, "For who has despised the day of small things?" (Zech. 4:10). These basic tenets provide small beginnings to a more abundant life. If they can do even the simplest thing like show up on time, and they see the reward of better relationships because of that, then the world begins to open up for them.

I had the divinely serendipitous opportunity to share these principles with some special kids in Africa. Through the ByGrace organization I ended up at a children's home in Nairobi. The kids were on school break. Many are orphans with no family to go home to over break. So they're stuck at the school.

I met brothers Chris and Peter, who were in high school. They had been living at ByGrace since they were young. Fortunately, they were rescued and now were students at the school. What impressed me was how emotionally articulate they all were. They were passionate about where they had come from, and how terrible it was, but they had a strong vision for their future.

I came back to the States, energized by their stories and hope-filled outlook. I decided not to buy Christmas presents for my family that year, but rather give (and encourage friends and family to give) to the organization making a new life possible for these kids.

I then learned of two other young men at the school named John and Alex. They too had their own heartbreaking stories—and had little or no support. I was so moved by all this that I committed to supporting some of them through college. We even held a silent auction at Brewer Direct and raised money for the school's science lab. These kids from rough backgrounds—who have so little and bless me with so much—they regularly get together to fast and pray just for me and my health issues. It's so humbling. We continue to dialogue in the most inspiring and heartfelt ways. At times, they actually call me Dad. Given their tumultuous family situations, I take this as an extremely touching honor.

Because I said yes, it's been such a blessing to be a blessing to them. What a witness to God's eternal grace to have their earthly grace poured out on me.

In my subsequent visits to Africa, I met Ann, Esther, James and Elvis. They too are all graduates of ByGrace. Each has his or her traumatic journey, but now, thank God, they all attend the university.

## Allan and His Ugandan Friends

On one of my Africa trips, I had an extra day in Uganda. Through my contacts with World Harvest, I met a wonderful man named Pastor Ndjoli. He works with pastors throughout east Africa—as well as promotes child sponsorship programs for needy families.

I met a young man named Allan. He, with his siblings, was struggling—working hard, doing whatever he could to get ahead in life. His father had left his mother for another woman. I got to know him and learned that he dreamed of going to a university and getting a degree.

So I asked Pastor Ndjoli if I could help mentor Allan through World Harvest. Of course, he was open to that.

Knowing the temptations that all young men face, especially one whose father played the field, I shared with Allan some advice about how to remain pure. I told him when the girls come around, be a gentleman. The friendship could easily slip into a physical relationship. I told him about the story of Sampson and Delilah and how his life, like Sampson, could be ruined with only one mistake.

I was also able to provide funding for Allan to realize his dream of going to college. In subsequent trips, I visited him at his college campus. What a thrill!

I also met and befriended other young people who are Allan's friends. Many did not have fathers. I completely identify with kids who don't have dads, because my dad was so distant. Even now they send me text messages. They call me Papa. They write, "Thank you for making me look smart"…"Thank you, Papa, for everything you do for me"…"I am more than happy and blessed by you"… "You made me feel loved"…"Such a joy getting to know you. My own blood Dad."

Again this is testament to God restoring the years the locust had eaten. What was missing in my childhood, hopefully in a small way, God is using to help shore up what is missing in these kids as well.

But the blessings didn't stop there. As an organization, Brewer Direct began sponsoring an 11-year-old child, Alvin, in Kamuli through World Harvest. I got a chance to return for a third trip to Africa. This boy and his impoverished family were so thankful. To show their gratitude they gave me a rooster to take back to California! Such encounters not only touch my heart, they're so much fun!

## Atsushi, Sayaka and My Many Japanese Friends

Earlier in my life, I promoted Japanese rock bands here in Los Angeles. Even though many of them have returned to Japan, I've remained in touch with them. They also threw a huge cancer-free party for me, after my surgery. These long-standing relationships have been so meaningful to me.

Many aren't believers. They know about my faith, but I tell them, "The fact that I believe in God won't change my relationship with you." They seem to appreciate the honesty. Of course I challenge them to consider the love that God has for them. They might just want to look into what Love itself offers. At times they don't respond. At other times I can tell they are open. But like Johnny Appleseed, I keep casting the seeds of life and truth that God provides. I say with no pretense, "I am here to help you with your spiritual life."

Some have had difficulties with their fathers and families. They're rebelling with the usual temptations of booze, cigarettes and women. Their compulsions certainly are a universal reality for many. It's my prayer that they'll discover the God who refers to himself as "Abba, Father." I was honored to officiate Atsushi and Sayaka's wedding. It was a beautiful affair. Atsushi's own father had died of cancer a few years back. Again, I could see the tapestry threads God was weaving, using my experience with cancer to relate to his tragic loss.

## Tommy and a Thailand Encounter

I find God moving in even the most mundane encounters. While in Thailand, I asked the hotel concierge for a restaurant recommendation, adding that I could not have spicy food as it would hurt my throat. Of course I explained, showing him the scar on my left forearm, the surgery I had gone through. His associate, Tommy, overheard the conversation. He stepped up and immediately told me that his sister just died from throat cancer only three months earlier.

Without missing a beat, I told him, "Tommy, I am here for you. God sent me to encourage you." In that simple moment, the world of truth and light once again shined. The Bible says we are not to hide our light under a basket. Why? Because there are lights within each person—often concealed—that are so eager and ready to come out. In one brief moment, eternity opened, and I was a conduit to reach out to another human being. We stayed in touch. I sent him a Bible and Christian CDs. Tragically, Tommy died of meningitis in 2016 at the age of 36. But I know he heard the Gospel.

There have been so many of these divine encounters. There was Yoshi, whom I met at a hotel lounge. He has since been added to my email list. I've told him, "The reason I'm in your life is to inspire you and to prod you to question your faith." I know he's listening. And it isn't just a one-way relationship. Yoshi helped with some Brewer Direct digital reporting, assisted me in getting a personal handle on social media and recommended a book that altered my thinking of my workweek.

There's Yota, who was manager at another hotel. After only a 15-minute exchange, he said he felt we should stay in touch. We have met for a two-hour dinner where we discussed everything from business, health and, of course, faith. We've promised to stay in touch, and next time I hope to meet his wife and family.

I like to think that I'm a spark, but God is the flame in these encounters. And boy do I love to see how God's truth and purposes begin to shine out through each of their lives. I can't even begin to write them all down. All I know is that as I am open, God opens hearts.

And isn't this what the Lord asks each of us to do? We don't stand, projecting a person who is perfect. We express, with open arms, what God has done. And we watch with eagerness the stirring of truth in someone else.

Every day I'm reminded of my brush with death. I actually have a permanent reminder "brushed" on my forearm. It's even brushed across my scratchy throat. Death wasn't a distant thing. No, it walked right up to me, and I was forced to trudge along with it.

But thankfully, God was gracious to push death back into the shadows. It was his grace that rescued me.

An amazing thing happened in that process, when the veil parted a little, and eternity loomed before me. I experienced a stripping away of falsities, distractions, little denials, foibles (I'm sure many would say, "Well not all of them, Randy")—the false person that I'm really not. And I received the incredible privilege of becoming acquainted with something quite special and unique: my true self.

But God is not content to let his amazing truths—his awakening of a true person—just be enjoyed and savored by the person himself. No, it is the nature of God, the ultimate Giver of Life, to prompt a person who has seen new light, to share that light. This isn't some rule or effort or striving. God forbid. I had enough of "should do" and "ought to" growing up. No, this light is so all-consuming, it can't help but spill out.

I often find myself being a gleeful observer of a divine choreographer. And I join the dance with other dance partners willingly. It is never arduous. The twin swords of condemnation and shame that would have prompted me in the past have truly been replaced by a new reality that brings life. It is a flame that doesn't go out. It fuels the human spirit. It is always on and never disappoints. It actually is born out of difficulty, if only to thumb its nose at anything that would pull you down. It's more than a candle in the dark. It is darkness nullified.

What is this thing?

It is the truth that stands between faith and love as a fulcrum.

It is the living reality called hope.

> ## "...a new heaven and a new earth..."
> Rev. 21:1

# Voice of Eternity

There is a Voice that speaks from eternity, calling all to come.

"And I heard a loud voice from the throne, saying, 'Behold, the tabernacle of God is among men, and He will dwell among them, and they shall be His people, and God Himself will be among them, and He will wipe away every tear from their eyes; and there will no longer be any death; there will no longer be any mourning, or crying, or pain; the first things have passed away'" (Rev. 21:3-4).

What a glorious Voice! A Voice capable of overcoming tears, death, mourning and pain.

This is our hope. Indeed, this is hope itself. There can be no other hope than this. For true hope is embodied in a person, Jesus Christ. He said in his final moments, "I go to prepare a place for you. If I go and prepare a place for you, I will come again and receive you to myself, that where I am, there you may be also" (John 14: 2-3).

The Voice from eternity, calling us to live forever, is our ultimate hope. It fuels our being here in this life. It is that very Voice that speaks through our voices, bringing life to all who are downcast. And that precious, powerful Voice will animate our being forever.

When the frailty of life causes us to falter, when we are attacked, persecuted or pulled down, when we face seemingly immovable obstacles, this Voice of Hope remains.

That Hope existed before time.

That Hope moves above and beyond our moments on earth.

That Hope will become our glorious reality forever.

# CHAPTER 11

# HOPE

---

"The cancer has returned."

When my doctor told me these words, it could have hit me like some horrible, mocking déjà vu. But strangely, that devastating sting of death just wasn't there.

A new CT scan revealed that the cancer had shown up in my lungs. The doctors showed me the little spots on the scan films. These miniscule dots had huge implications. They could grow. They could overtake this healthy organ and eventually others as well. And of course, they could kill.

To make matters worse, the kind of cancer I have is not treatable by chemo or radiation. (Not that I would want to go through that anyway.) And the spots are too tiny and too many to operate on and remove.

Once again, I am looking at disease and death in the face, and with it, potential devastating despair.

But now there's a simple yet powerful difference. I am living and breathing and even fueled by this thing called hope. It also has manifested itself in real ways. The Bible says that "hope does not disappoint." That is certainly the case.

My life now centers on that wonderful truth in the old hymn by Edward Mote, "My hope is built on nothing less, than Jesus' blood and righteousness. I dare not trust the sweetest frame, but wholly lean on Jesus' name. On Christ the solid rock I stand, all other ground is sinking sand."

The doctors are trying other new treatments. So far, none has been effective. I guess you could say, the verdict is still out. My future is unsure. But this uncertainty does not cause me to spiral downward.

Why? Because I've learned an amazing thing about this phenomenon called hope. Now I don't just trust it if things will turn out okay. Hope is a buoy that operates *despite* circumstance. In other words, you might try to submerge a buoy. You may even drive it beneath the surface. But it always pops back up. Hope will always find the surface—the light, the air. And that buoyancy is ever-present within me. As one of my friends said, "A lot of people say they are blessed and fortunate when everything is going well. You've shown that you can experience the joy and grace of God when things aren't so easy."

This is the nature of hope. The Bible says that through faith it provides confident assurance: "Now faith is confidence in what we hope for and assurance about what we do not see" (Heb. 11:1).

But that word *confidence* is more than just pumped-up self-reliance. The word in Greek is *hypostasis*. It is actually a word commonly used by ancient Greek authors including Aristotle. It literally means, "a setting or placing under...a substructure...a foundation." The King James Version translates the word as "substance" or "that which has actual existence—a real thing!"

In other words, true hope is not simply wishful thinking. It isn't dream-casting or some would-be, wannabe, out-in-the-clouds happenstance. True hope truly exists because it's based on the one who is hope himself.

As a professional fundraiser, I see many good causes worthy of donations. People worldwide are endeavoring to heal the planet, save the whales, feed the hungry and help the poor, among other things. They are all worthy causes, and those involved are to be admired. But it's hope that differentiates eternal purposes from simply good causes. I have come to say, doing good isn't good enough. Without the element of hope in God and his eternal purposes, it is all window dressing.

Will we ever lift people out of homelessness or addiction?

Some people say, "Well, I hope so," as if hope is a maybe or, "If we are lucky." But when we apply true hope to the challenge of overcoming poverty, homelessness, and addiction, we move from a flip shrug to a fervent passion. In working with so many homeless missions over the years, I've seen firsthand the programs that bring about real change. They don't just offer Band-Aids and hand pats. They offer *hypostasis*—real confidence, real foundation, real substance, and real, life-changing hope that a homeless person or an addict can actually rebuild their life.

I find hope for the future when I encounter true faith-first charities—those whose core purpose is eternal and to proclaim Jesus until he comes again (whether in word or deed, or both). Jeremiah 29:11 says, "'For I know the plans that I have for you,' declares the Lord, 'plans for welfare and not for calamity to give you a future and a hope.'" Hope for those being served. Hope for something better, greater. Hope in the glory of God.

True hope operates out in front of us. But it also works *under* us to support us. (*Hypo,* in the Greek, literally means "under.") Think of it this way: Hope is a lighthouse that ushers all ships to safe harbor. It is a guiding light. But it is so much more than simply a beacon. It has a life and internal light of its own. In addition to being the light before us, it's the fire that fuels us. Hope is also the engine that guides the ship to safe harbor. In other words, hope gives us the assurance, expectation, confidence and conviction of a thing we see in the future. But even as we move toward that thing we hope for, we are strengthened and fueled by hope. Hope beacons us and bolsters us at the same time!

Now as I move to the next chapter in my life, I find that, indeed, hope operates in this duel fashion. It has become both an anchor and the wind in my sails. It gives me security, and it also fills me, taking me to new vistas. In fact, the Bible refers to hope as an anchor: "We have this hope as anchor for the soul, firm and secure" (Heb. 6:19).

I'm moved by songs like Andraé Crouch's, "I've Got Confidence." Its lyrics "I'm tossed from side to side" captures my emotions as I too "can't tell my night from day." And yet, as the lyrics go, "I've got confidence." Yes, God will see me through.

One of the most upside-down, seemingly contradictory things about hope is that it is born by its polar opposite. It comes when we are facing hopeless situations. The Bible states: "Not only so, but we also glory in our sufferings, because we know that suffering produces perseverance; perseverance, character; and character, hope. And hope does not put us to shame, because God's love has been poured out into our hearts through the Holy Spirit, who has been given to us" (Rom. 5:3-5). In the midst of life's most difficult encounters, hope is revealed—greeting us like a faithful companion, emboldening us like a strong champion.

It's as though hope dares darkness to squelch the light. Hope asserts that it can overcome the blackest situation. Indeed, it can turn dark to light, difficulty to success, death to life. Like a skilled judo wrestler, it will use the very power of hardship against itself, bringing victory.

Hope also operates like the sequoia tree. The seeds only come out of the pod if there is fire. The grand, glorious trees that grow to enormous heights and live for over a thousand years are birthed by flames—the thing that normally destroys.

Adversity, in my case, could be met by cynicism—"See Randy, you weren't really healed." But hope turns that mocking scorn on its ear. Hope scoffs at its would-be scoffers. Hope says to the mayhem of life, "Give me your best shot, and I will replace it with God's best in return."

I can say this with confidence, because I've seen it operate firsthand in my life. The worst life could offer has been turned into the best God intended. Is there any greater reason to hope?!

I see and bear witness to the fact that God has turned my bad for good, even the tremendous dysfunctions of my youth. The Bible says, "...but where sin increased, grace abounded all the more..." (Rom. 5:20). And I am experiencing that in greater and greater measure.

My parents barely left the little town of El Monte while I travel the world, like Johnny Appleseed, sewing God's seeds of goodness. Worse, my parents were never able to leave or abandon condemnation and shame. But through God's undeserved provision, I have been blessed not only to understand the truth of grace and hope, but now in my own small way, I am grace and hope's ambassador. It is a testament to God's amazing power, not my own. I wouldn't be in a place to speak, if cancer hadn't birthed my voice.

I live and move on wings of eagles. The verses found in Isaiah 40:30-31 are true on a daily basis: "Even youths grow tired and weary, and young men stumble and fall; but those who hope in the

Lord *will* renew their strength. They *will* soar on wings like eagles; they *will* run and not grow weary, they *will* walk and not faint."

Again, hope is shown *not* to be a fickle friend. It boldly asserts confidence and firm conviction. After hoping in the Lord, things *will* happen. Hope *will* renew strength, cause us to soar like eagles, run and not grow weary, and walk and not faint. Hope isn't a matter of a trumped-up human will. It is a by-product—a reality brought to life—of an eternal will that has infused us with hope.

I don't feel defeated. Defeat is not a physical thing. It's a spiritual and mental reality. I know every story may not have a happy ending. But through God's grace, I can see miracles along the way. Once again, I believe God has brought me to this place, so that he can show himself strong through me; and that I can be healed. I believe he made provision for my healing in the body of Jesus at the cross. I believe that by his scourging, we are healed. "But he was pierced through for our transgressions, he was crushed for our iniquities; The chastening for our well-being fell upon Him, and by His scourging we are healed" (Isa. 53:5). But until that happens physically, I will continue to be grace, hope and healing for other people.

I tell myself again and again: *My hope is built on nothing less than Jesus' blood and righteousness. I dare not trust the sweetest frame, but wholly lean on Jesus' name.*

If, however, it goes the other way, I can't lose. It's good either way. There is an assurance I will not be disappointed. Hope isn't an object of our faith. It's a living thing within our faith. I have found purpose specifically in helping young people get into college and complete their education. At times I've been led to play a surrogate father financially, but more importantly in helping them overcome their feelings of abandonment and dissipated purpose. This is the nature of grace—of "all things working together for good." God did not intend for my parents to inflict the darkness they did on me. But through his grace he used it to make his light shine even greater and to show others who have suffered like me that same possibility of grace.

A new chapter has begun. Some would say it is dark and foreboding. Others might scoff, "So much for that 'miracle' healing." But if the evidence of truth is freedom, then I can say with unswerving conviction, there has been a real, abiding and liberating change in not just my outlook, but in the very core of my being. The truth is, I have been set free.

The evidence of this is how I am dealing with these set-backs. In my new moments, I'm surrounded in this amazing awareness and comfort: an expectation that all not only will be—but *is*—okay. This isn't a frivolous, "Oh well." No, when death came and went, what miraculously was left behind was an abiding hope. The newly emerged, or expanded Randy, is seeing things with a greater vibrancy. At Brewer Direct, we've always included the idea of hope in our marketing and fund-raising packages to inspire donors to help homeless missions and other worthy outreaches. Now hope has taken on a whole new meaning.

Don't get me wrong. I'm not happy about these new health challenges. I'm not happy about regularly getting stuck with needles and running endless tests. But beneath, or rather beyond circumstantial happiness is this treasure—this deep well—that I can draw from. True hope is just that: it comes in endless supply that never runs out. It is an eternal spring of confidence. I'm held by something infinitely bigger than myself. I am not outside the things of the earth, but rather, more fully realized even as I walk through them.

Each day, with every utterance, I know that my physical voice has been spared. More importantly I know the distinctive Voice within—that was fashioned before I was even born and will live even when I die—has found its true resonance. The authentic Randy lives! I humbly stand in awe that all of this has been given to me—yes, given—without any requirement on my part. All I had to do was accept the free gift God gave— Jesus himself. I know that whatever shout or whisper, whatever voice I have, is all because of this oil of grace poured over me, by the giver of grace himself. In all this, my very core lives and moves and has its being, fueled by the eternal flame of hope.

I am a distinct voice, a unique utterance, a forever expression of God's grace, hope and healing. God gave me the gift of the sound of my voice. But it's more than just a physical voice. There's a spiritual dimension to it. The Bible says, "I have been crucified with Christ; and it is no longer I who live, but Christ who lives in me; and the life which I now live in the flesh I live by faith in the Son of God, who loved me and gave himself up for me" (Gal. 2:20). His Spirit and mine have become one, and that Spirit within me is spoken in and through me. There is nothing more exhilarating and life-giving than to live out this reality with the words that come out of my mouth. I am Christ living through me, speaking to those in the world that come across my path.

I know that God desires this for you. You are an exceptionally unique person that God knew before you were even born. As you invite God in, he will be about the work of making that distinctive Voice fully realized. His divine imprint within you will live out through you in unimaginable ways. You too can be your own forever expression of God's grace, hope and healing. Wherever you are today, whatever your situation, know with confidence that your faith in God can be trusted.

Therefore, have hope!

# "...the least of these..."

Matt 25:40

# VOICE TO THE HURTING

The Voice becomes action.

Jesus asked us to be an expression to the world, not just through our physical speech, but through hands and feet.

We are to be an outpouring of love to the hungry, the thirsty, the stranger, the naked, the imprisoned—all who are downtrodden—all who suffer.

Today, we label them the homeless, the addicted, the down-and-out.

These outcasts are deemed precious by Jesus who lived in many ways like an outcast. He had no place to lay his head. He had no earthly treasure. In spite of this, he saw each of these hurting people as living treasures, despite all outward appearances or compulsions or personal failure.

Jesus called them the "least of these." But he bid us to treat them with the greatest outpouring of love and care.

He wants us to turn heartache to hearts fulfilled, strung out to knit together, hungry to satisfied, imprisoned to free, lost to found.

There will be eternal blessing to those who do this. But also there is the real earthly blessing that it's better to give than receive. Lifting up a broken life, lifts all to places of unspeakable joy.

The voices of the hurting are inviting us to turn words to action. In blessing them, we help create not just a new melody in their hearts; but we recognize a wonderful, eternal song in our own.

# FOR THOSE WHO HAVE LOST HOPE

---

Grace, hope and healing are often overused, misunderstood or even trivialized concepts. If you're feeling utterly hopeless, or sensing that God's grace is not for you or doesn't even exist, or if you're feeling entangled in cynicism about the very idea that God can heal you—then *hopefully* these words will restore you once again.

## Grace

"For the Law was given through Moses; grace and truth were realized through Jesus Christ" (John 1:17).

"The Law came in so that the transgression would increase; but where sin increased, grace abounded all the more…" (Rom. 5:20).

"And He has said to me, 'My grace is sufficient for you, for power is perfected in weakness.' Most gladly, therefore, I will rather boast about my weaknesses, so that the power of Christ may dwell in me" (2 Cor. 12:9).

"For by grace you have been saved through faith; and that not of yourselves, it is the gift of God..." (Eph. 2:8).

"Let your speech always be with grace, as though seasoned with salt, so that you will know how you should respond to each person" (Col. 4:6).

"But he gives a greater grace. Therefore, it says, 'God is opposed to the proud, but gives grace to the humble'" (Jas. 4:6).

"... when I am weak, then I am strong" (2 Cor. 12:10).

"All things work together for good" (Rom. 8:28).

"You have taken account of my wanderings; Put my tears in Your bottle. Are they not in Your book? This I know, that God is for me. For You have delivered my soul from death. So that I may walk before God in the light of the living" (Ps. 56:8-13).

"Let your gentle spirit be known to all men. The Lord is near" (Phil. 4:5).

"... ready to make a defense to everyone who asks you to give an account for the hope that is in you, yet with gentleness and reverence" (1 Pet. 3:15).

"Now faith is confidence in what we hope for and assurance about what we do not see" (Heb. 11:1).

## Hope

"'For I know the plans that I have for you,' declares the Lord, 'plans for welfare and not for calamity to give you a future and a hope'" (Jer. 29:11).

"Sing to the Lord a new song; sing to the Lord, all the earth" (Ps . 96:1).

"We have this hope as anchor for the soul, firm and secure" (Heb. 6:19).

"Not only so, but we also glory in our sufferings, because we know that suffering produces perseverance; perseverance, character; and character, hope. And hope does not put us to shame, because God's love has been poured out into our hearts through the Holy Spirit, who has been given to us" (Rom. 5:3-5).

"Even youths grow tired and weary, and young men stumble and fall; but those who hope in the Lord will renew their strength. They will soar on wings like eagles; they will run and not grow weary, they will walk and not be faint" (Isa. 40:30-31).

"Be strong and let your heart take courage, all you who hope in the Lord" (Ps. 31:24).

"For I hope in You, O Lord; You will answer, O Lord my God" (Ps. 38:15).

"My soul, wait in silence for God only, for my hope is from Him" (Ps. 62:5).

"But as for me, I will hope continually…" (Ps. 71:14).

"I wait for the Lord, my soul does wait, and in His word do I hope" (Ps. 130:5).

"How blessed is he whose help is the God of Jacob, whose hope is in the Lord his God…" (Ps. 146:5).

"In hope against hope he believed, so that he might become a father of many nations…" (Rom. 4:18).

"For in hope we have been saved, but hope that is seen is not hope; for who hopes for what he already sees? But if we hope for what we do not see, with perseverance we wait eagerly for it" (Rom. 8:24-25).

"Now may the God of hope fill you with all joy and peace in believing, so that you will abound in hope by the power of the Holy Spirit" (Rom. 15:13).

"...love bears all things, believes all things, hopes all things, endures all things." (1 Cor. 13:7).

"I pray that the eyes of your heart may be enlightened, so that you will know what is the hope of His calling, what are the riches of the glory of His inheritance in the saints...." (Eph. 1:18).

"Now faith is the assurance of things hoped for, the conviction of things not seen" Heb. 11:1).

## Healing

"As He passed by, He saw a man blind from birth. And His disciples asked Him, 'Rabbi, who sinned, this man or his parents, that he would be born blind?' Jesus answered, 'It was neither that this man sinned, nor his parents; but it was so that the works of God might be displayed in him. We must work the works of Him who sent Me as long as it is day; night is coming when no one can work. While I am in the world, I am the Light of the world.' When He had said this, He spat on the ground, and made clay of the spittle, and applied the clay to his eyes, and said to him, 'Go, wash in the pool of Siloam' (which is translated, Sent). So he went away and washed, and came back seeing. Therefore, the neighbors, and those who previously saw him as a beggar, were saying, 'Is not this the one who used to sit and beg?' Others were saying, 'This is he,' still others were saying, 'No, but he is like him.' He kept saying, 'I am the one.' So they were saying to him, 'How then were your eyes opened?' He answered, 'The man who is called Jesus made clay, and anointed my eyes, and said to me, "Go to Siloam and wash"; so I went away and washed, and I received sight'" (John 9:1-11).

"But He was pierced through for our transgressions, He was crushed for our iniquities; The chastening for our well-being fell upon Him, and by His scourging we are healed" (Isa. 53:5).

"...for I, the Lord, am your healer" (Exod. 15:20).

"... 'See now that I, I am He, and there is no god besides Me; It is I who put to death and give life. I have wounded and it is I who heal'..." (Deut. 32:39).

"I have heard your prayer, I have seen your tears; behold, I will heal you" (2 Kings 20:5).

"O Lord my God, I cried to You for help, and You healed me" (Ps. 30:2).

"The Lord will sustain him upon his sickbed; In his illness, you restore him to health" (Ps. 41:3).

"Who pardons all your iniquities, who heals all your diseases..." (Ps. 103:3).

"... 'For I will restore you to health and I will heal you of your wounds,' declares the Lord..." (Jer 30:17).

"But for you who fear My name, the sun of righteousness will rise with healing in its wings..." (Mal. 4:2).

"Jesus was going throughout all Galilee, teaching in their synagogues and proclaiming the gospel of the kingdom, and healing every kind of disease and every kind of sickness among the people" (Matt. 4:23).

"And large crowds came to Him, bringing with them those who were lame, crippled, blind, mute, and many others, and they laid them down at His feet; and He healed them." (Matt. 15:30).

"And He said to her, 'Daughter, your faith has made you well; go in peace and be healed of your affliction'" (Mark 5:34).

"And all the people were trying to touch Him, for power was coming from Him and healing them all" (Luke 6:19).

"Therefore, confess your sins to one another, and pray for one another so that you may be healed. The effective prayer of a righteous man can accomplish much" (Jas. 5:16).

"Beloved, I pray that in all respects you may prosper and be in good health, just as your soul prospers" (3 John 2).

"On either side of the river was the tree of life, bearing twelve kinds of fruit, yielding its fruit every month; and the leaves of the tree were for the healing of the nations" (Rev. 22:2).

## And here is my favorite verse, encompassing and covering all.

"And we know that God causes all things to work together for good to those who love God, to those who are called according to His purpose" (Rom. 8:28).

Made in the USA
Las Vegas, NV
30 October 2023

79943334R00068